Two Bills
from
Boston

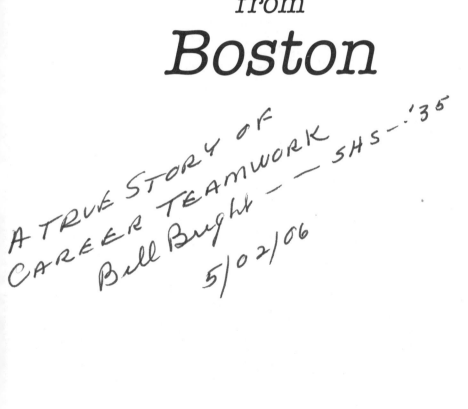

A TRUE STORY OF
CAREER TEAMWORK — SHS — '35
Bill Bright
5/02/06

Two *Bills* from *Boston*

Making the American Dream Come True

Bill Bright

BookPartners
Wilsonville, Oregon

Library of Congress Cataloging-in-Publication Data

Bright, Bill, 1917–
    Two Bills from Boston : making the American dream come true /
Bill Bright.
       p. cm.
    ISBN 1-581-51049-7 (pb : alk.paper)
    1. Western Power Products--History. 2. Electric industries--United
States--History. 3. Bright, Bill, 1917– 4. Wild, Bill, 1917–1983. 5.
Industrialists--United States--Biography. 6. Entrepreneurship--United
States--Case studies. 7. Success in business--United States--Case
studies. I. Title.

    HD9697.A3 U524 1999
    338.7'62131042'092--dc21
    [B]

                           99-044987

Copyright © 2000 by William Bright
All rights reserved
Printed in U.S.A.

Cover design by Richard Ferguson
Text design by Sheryl Mehary

This book may not be reproduced in whole or in part, by
electronic or any other means which exist or may yet be
developed, without permission of:

BookPartners, Inc.
P. O. Box 922
Wilsonville, Oregon 97070

Dedication

I wish to thank the many people who offered help, advice, and encouragement to me through the years of my career; but in particular I wish to dedicate the book to the three individuals most responsible for the successful conclusion of my lifelong career goals.

To my mother, Anna C. Bright, who stitched shoes in a factory to support our family after my father passed away. Her advice to me was to choose a lifetime career as early in life as possible, and to work hard and smart toward achieving my career goal.

To my pal, William F. Wild. Together, at age eighteen, we formulated a "management-friendly" work plan, coupled with night school classes. This allowed us to advance rapidly to supervisory positions, and to help each other over the years to achieve our separate career goals. Bill was always there when I needed help, as I was for him. The fact that we both succeeded as planned underlines my admiration for this great guy.

To my wonderful wife, Joan Robinette Bright, who was actively involved in the growth and operation of our company. She was "at home" with employees, staff, and customers. She participated in every board of directors meeting, traveled with me and was involved in customer marketing meetings across the United States and in foreign countries. Joan contributed her talents to the preparation of *Two Bills from Boston,* including typing of manuscripts and computer work. Our operation of the company was indeed interesting, challenging, and fun for both of us.

Contents

Introduction

This is the story of two young men named Bill who set out on life during the Great Depression, with no money for college. But they were determined to find a way to advance in their jobs, save their money, and achieve their career goals.

Bill Wild set his sights on becoming an executive in a large corporation involved in interesting electrical work, and eventually on a comfortable retirement. Bill Bright visualized a career in the electrical industry as an entrepreneur, building his own manufacturing company.

To pursue their visions of success, the two eighteen-year-old Bills developed a teamwork plan which included a management-friendly work attitude designed to convince their employers of their desire to advance. Their plan also included night study in engineering classes as an after-work priority.

The team effort of the two Bills produced spectacular results. They worked together for eleven years, establishing work standards that guided them in the following years to their career goals.

Their work plan originated from advice Bright's Uncle Bill gave him a year before young Bill's high school graduation: "The most important thing for a young person to remember when starting a career is the work ethic. Attract management's attention by hard work. Be interested, ask questions, take night study courses, and let people know you want to advance."

Years later, an observation by B. C. Forbes gave further emphasis to Uncle Bill's advice:

"Tell me how a young man spends his evenings, and I will tell you how far he is likely to go in the world. The popular notion is that a youth's progress depends upon how he utilizes his leisure. If he spends it in harmless idleness, he is likely to be kept on the payroll, but that will be about all. If he diligently utilizes his own time to fit himself for more responsible duties, then the greater responsibilities—and the greater rewards—are almost certain to come to him."

Their management-friendly work ethic attracted their employers' attention during their first jobs in a machine shop, resulting in an offer of electrical jobs in shipbuilding. They advanced rapidly because of their unusual work attitude, and within six years Bright had reached the top electrical position building ships for the U.S. Navy, and Wild had risen to electrical shop superintendent, and later to general manager of ship repair.

After shipbuilding and a U.S. Army enlistment, Bill Bright accepted a position as a sales engineer representing manufacturers of equipment used by electric utilities. This sales and marketing activity would prepare him for a career as an entrepreneur, building his own company for the development and manufacture of products for the electric utility industry.

Bill Wild made his career decision to remain in the shipbuilding/ship repair industry, advancing to general manager of a ship repair facility in San Diego, California.

This book will help readers seeking advancement to jobs of higher responsibility, whether they plan a career in sales and engineering or as an entrepreneur. I hope you will find helpful guidance in taking the steps necessary for success in your demanding but rewarding life work.

1

Envisioning a Career

The year was 1935. I had my diploma from Saugus High School in Massachusetts—my first career goal achieved. Like so many other families of high school graduates during the Great Depression years, mine had no money to help me with college tuition and expenses. Student loans were nonexistent in those days. Thousands of factory workers had lost their jobs, and the prospects that a high school graduate would find work were very slim.

I grew up in the town of Saugus, about ten miles northeast of Boston. It was primarily a bedroom community for people working in Boston or in the adjacent city of Lynn, where General Electric had two large factories. Both GE factories had drastically reduced the number of their employees. The shoe industry in Lynn had once been recognized as a national production center with several large factories, leather tanneries, and shoe machinery manufacturers. Almost all had closed. The factories had been dispersed to other states after a series of strikes by labor unions.

Before I could start college, I had to to find a job and save some money. The previous two years I had worked summers for two local florist companies. Donovan's grew giant pansies and other annuals. I worked at their nursery on weekends, in the greenhouse with Mrs.

Donovan, and waited on customers who purchased seedlings, shrubs and other plants at the outdoor display area alongside the turnpike.

The other florist was Cogger's, where I worked during the week in the fields with Steve Stevenson as my boss. Both Mrs. Donovan and Steve treated me very well. The work in the fields was hard and dirty, but the money was good. Steve kept up a constant chatter as we worked, mostly about his two favorite subjects—his fiancée, Florence, and high school football. I played tackle for our high school team, and Steve was there on the sidelines at every game, yelling at the team. He knew the names of all of our players and knew every team in the conference. He talked football for hours, all without pausing for a moment in his hoeing, weeding, or transplanting.

My only employment option after graduation was to try to get my old jobs back. The summer would give me more time to investigate other job prospects and plan my career.

It was quite different that year, working in the fields for Donovan's and Cogger's after graduation. I thought about which companies in Boston to contact for a job, after my eighteenth birthday in September.

I really had been thinking about a career since entering high school. My elective subjects included chemistry, advanced math, physics and Latin—preparation for college entrance and a major in electrical engineering.

My choice of a career as an electrical engineer was not a snap judgment. Mother and I had had many discussions about careers during my school years. She stressed the importance of my investigating as many career choices as possible to find work that would be interesting and challenging, with a promising future. She urged me to talk with adults to find out if they liked their jobs, and why. Many times my mother said, "A person with no lifetime career goal is like a leaf floating on a stream, moving wherever the current and wind takes it, and ending up forever on whatever rock or beach it comes to rest on. No way would you want that kind of future."

Although I did talk with many adults about their jobs, I found very few who could say they really liked their lifetime work. Most seemed to be working strictly to support a family.

I know the career question was already in my mind by the age of fourteen. At that time I thought the ideal career would be with the U.S. Navy. My brother-in-law Ben was the radio operator on a large fishing fleet trawler. Knowing of my interest in the Navy, he invited me along on a two-week voyage to George's Banks off the coast of Maine. The first week, I was seasick enough to convince me a Navy career was not my first choice.

Many of my friends worked part time on farms while in high school and praised the farmer's uncomplicated lifestyle, the fresh air, and the closeness to nature. I was friendly with a son of a local farmer and often helped him with his chores after school. A lot of the work was really fun. However, this work went on every day from before dawn until dark, winter and summer. Farming would not be my career choice.

Another possibility I considered, following the lead of several of my ancestors, was carpentry. The opportunity to try it came when I was in the eighth grade. A disaster occurred one snowy February morning: our house was destroyed by fire. Father had passed away three years earlier. My brother George had left home for work in Boston, and my sister Annie had married. At the time of the fire, living at home with Mother were my two sisters, Dorothy and Frances, and myself as "man of the house."

A friend and neighbor who was a carpenter by trade offered to rebuild our house for the amount of our insurance money, if I would be his helper. During construction of the house, he taught me carpentry skills that I have used throughout my life. Although the work was interesting, I considered it limited in potential as a career choice.

When the partitions were in place and the shell of the house was finished, I told the carpenter I wanted to do the electrical wiring. We checked the rules and found that a homeowner could wire his own house, but a licensed electrician had to install the service entrance wiring to the fuse panel. Mr. Pike, a local electrician, cooperated. I checked a book out of the Saugus Public Library, purchased all the material required, and did the entire job. Everything was according to code, and the inspector could find nothing wrong.

I had been fascinated by electricity since it was first installed in our original home. As a young boy, I shared with my sister Frances the daily task of filling the lamps with kerosene, trimming wicks and polishing the chimneys. I will never forget the amazement and delight of turning on those first electric lights. Touching a wall switch would turn night into day. I knew, after finishing the wiring of our new house at age fourteen, that I would work to find some way to become involved in the electrical industry as a career.

I discussed my plans for the future after graduation with many of our family friends and contacts. I received some well-intended advice, generally pointing toward the realities of life in our small town. A typical comment went, "Well, if I were you, I would concentrate on finding a good steady job. To be an engineer you need a college degree. To go to college you need lots of money. Even with a steady job, it will take many years to save enough money for four years of college. Better use your energy to find steady work."

My boss Steve and I had several conversations about my future plans. He agreed with my ambitious plan to find a steady job, study engineering subjects at night, work toward an engineering future, and someday build my own business. He encouraged me to contact him any summer I needed a job. I set the date to quit the nursery job as the last day of work in August so that I could go job-hunting right after my birthday, September 3.

I could always find part-time work during my high school years. Employers would hire me because I seemed to enjoy hard work. Hard work produced the following big career boost.

"Hey Bill," Steve said to me one day during our lunch break, "have you ever put in a job application at General Electric Company?"

"Gosh no, Steve, GE has laid off thousands of people. The last few times I've walked by the West Lynn Works, there were a few hundred guys out on the sidewalk and in the street waiting for their names to be called for part-time work. Not much point of applying there till things pick up," I said.

"Look, there were a lot of guys ahead of you in football when you started, but you worked at it and made varsity. Who knows when business will pick up again? We both know that if you don't at least stop in at the employment department and make out an application, you'll never get called, if and when they get busy," he said, giving me a stern look.

"So okay, the first work day after my eighteenth birthday, I'll get in there and do it."

I thought to myself that it was a hopeless exercise. Sure, I'd walk down to the West Lynn Works, and probably not be able to get through to the gate. Then, if I could get inside, they'd tell me they were not hiring and wouldn't know when they would start hiring. But I did promise Steve, so I'd do it.

On a Wednesday morning, the day after my eighteenth birthday, I dressed in my best clothes—new haircut and all—and set out on the four-mile walk down Walnut Street, along Birch Pond, past the barn where the National Guard kept their well-groomed horses. I paused briefly to check them over as they loafed in the corral. Finally I arrived at the General Electric Company West Lynn Works, complete with the expected crowd of laid-off workers in front of the massive iron gate blocking the entrance to the plant.

The crowd was almost all men, standing shoulder to shoulder, crowded as closely as possible near the front, eager to be the first called in for part-time work. These were pretty desperate people, out of work for many weeks, and probably most had families to care for, and with savings gone, they would take any kind of a job.

I made my way through the mob very carefully and politely, asking people if I could squeeze through. Before long I was close enough to the iron gate to yell over to the guard that I had been told to report to the employment office. (This was the truth, because Steve had told me to.) The guard walked over, opened the pedestrian gate and motioned me to enter. He escorted me into the employment office.

Once inside the employment office, the guard turned me over to the receptionist and left. I told her that I would like to make out an employment application. She was very nice and handed me a form to fill out, pointed to a chair and table, and said to return the completed form to her.

As references, I listed people for whom I had worked, including Steve. Behind the counter were several women busily working at desks, and behind them were offices, with everything neat and orderly. The only sound was the clatter of typewriters.

Even though I felt that this job application procedure was an exercise in futility, it was a thrill for me to be inside a large manufacturing plant, and to be an adult at last, with a high school diploma in hand, applying for a real job.

2

Two Bills at General Electric

The receptionist read through the completed application form, then turned around and yelled, "Hey Florence, your applicant!" A very attractive woman left her desk and came over to me.

"Well, Mr. Bright, you've been highly recommended. Follow me," she said.

I realized that this young woman had to be Steve's girlfriend, Florence. Steve had never mentioned where Florence worked. This was clearly a set-up to surprise me. I was flabbergasted. Florence, never mentioning Steve, turned me over to a woman in another office. All I could do was stutter a thank you. What a wonderful thing Steve and Florence did for me—a break beyond my wildest dreams! Steve had recommended me, and Florence had risked recommending me, not because I had played football, but probably because of my hard work and my plans for the future.

The interview went fine. The interviewer wanted to know about high school subjects and grades, job experiences, and plans for the future. Then she had some gadgets for me to assemble. Some were simple puzzles, such as placing variously shaped wood blocks into their proper holes. Then she took me to another office where I was given more forms to fill out.

As the interviewer left with my finished forms, she told me to read some employee newsletters while waiting for another person to take over my interview. After an hour or so, a man entered the office and introduced himself as a supervisor.

"Mr. Bright, I want to welcome you as a new employee of General Electric Company. Report here to me next Monday morning at seven-thirty for a temporary assignment to the watt-hour meter department, to fill in for a vacationing employee," he said.

This series of events left me wondering if I was dreaming. I found my way back through the office to the guard, who motioned me through the personnel gate and into the crowd. Thanks to Steve and Florence, my second career goal had been accomplished. With a good job and money coming in, I could now enroll in night engineering courses at Franklin Union Technical Institute in Boston.

The next Monday morning I was waiting at G.E. for the supervisor in his office at seven-fifteen. He finally showed up, and we walked through the plant to the watt-hour meter department, where he introduced me to the foreman.

The foreman told me, in summary, "All power companies install watt-hour meters wherever customers use electricity, so that the exact amount of electricity used can be billed monthly. General Electric is one of the world leaders in the development and production of the watt-hour meter. Many of the components of the meter are manufactured right here at the West Lynn Works." The fact that new customers for electricity continued to increase even during the Great Depression explained why the West Lynn Works continued to be busy in the departments that were involved with watt-hour meters.

After the discussion we moved into the assembly room, which featured a long bench lined with two or three dozen stools, spaced about four feet apart. A moving belt traveled across the full length of the bench. On a wall behind the bench and in front of each stool were a number of small bins, each containing a different part of a watt-hour meter.

Various tools—electric screwdrivers, soldering irons, and so on—were suspended by springs attached to the ceiling over the bench and in front of each stool. The room was well lighted and very clean, with a controlled temperature. Soon the workers, all women, came in and sat down on their stools. The belt started up at 8:00 a.m., and the assembly line began.

This had to be the most boring job in the plant, but fortunately it was only temporary for me. The week soon ended, and Friday became my first G.E. payday. A supervisor came by at quitting time and handed me a small brown envelope containing my week's pay, in cash—the law in those days.

"Here's your pay. Report Monday to Mr. Hooper in the screw machine department. Thanks for helping out and good luck," he said.

When Monday morning came, I was waiting at 7:15 for the office to open. Mr. Hooper, my supervisor in the screw machine department, came in sometime later. His office was glass-enclosed and located on one side of a large manufacturing space. Directly across the floor and aisle from his office was the header department, where bolts were made. Adjacent to his office was the screw machine department. There was a sort of smoky smell of hot oil, typical in areas with lots of operating machinery.

Mr. Hooper showed up nicely dressed in white shirt, jacket and tie. He was a fiftyish, bald man of moderate stature, and very well-mannered. He welcomed me to the department with a big smile, saying I had been highly recommended (probably by Steve via Florence), and proceeded to introduce me to several office people, including the foreman, Mr. Allen.

Following a tour of the screw machine department, where many meter components were manufactured, we came to the header department where, Mr. Hooper explained, nuts and bolts were produced. Along with the thirty or forty header machines in the department, there were also lathes, drill presses, grinders, threading machines and other equipment.

After the tour, Mr. Hooper turned me over to Mr. Allen, who would teach me to be a header machine operator, as well as how to operate the lathes, drill presses, grinders, and associated equipment. Mr. Allen was a tall, pleasant man in his late thirties. He was very friendly from the start and an excellent teacher.

My battery of four headers were located across the aisle from the foreman's desk, and he promised all the help I would need. He explained, "The header machine cuts a short length of wire from a coil, and forms a bolt head on one end. The bolt head can be produced flat, or round or hexagonal, and at blinding speed. The bolt has threads and a slot for a screwdriver blade installed by separate machines."

The noise level of the header machines in operation was unbelievably high. It was necessary to shout within a few inches of a person's ear to be heard during the work day. As Mr. Allen was trying to outshout the noise of the headers to explain the function of some highly accurate measuring instruments, all the headers suddenly stopped operating. The eerie silence made me conscious of the ringing in my ears. It was time for lunch.

My brown-bag lunch was handy, and I went over to join a few of the men who were sitting on a bench along a wall as they ate their lunches and visited. I was starting to get acquainted with my fellow workers when suddenly someone whacked me on my back. Turning around, I saw Bill Wild, a classmate at Saugus High School. What a surprise and relief to find another person of my age in the department! All of the other operators were older men.

Bill was grinning from ear to ear. With his arm around my shoulders, he guided me to his favorite lunch spot near a source of hot coffee and soft drinks. In addition to the beverages, there was a candy bar machine that dispensed an extra bar free if the purchaser was aware of a little trick Bill shared with me.

Bill was my age, height, and build. He had black hair—a nice looking guy, very cheerful and outgoing, usually with a half grin and sparkle in his eye—a contrast to my blond hair and more reserved personality. We had never been friendly during high school, simply because we were from different parts of town. Also, I played football, while Bill played baseball, we each tended to pal around with our own teammates.

"Hey, how did you ever manage to get a job here?" Bill asked.

"Well, I had a friend who had a friend in the company. They put in a good word for me. So how about you, how did you get hired?" I said.

"Well, my dad has worked here for a long time. He's in charge of the West Lynn Works electrical system. He put in a good word for me, too."

Friday was payday. Several of the men would go to a favorite restaurant a few blocks away on Lynn Common. Bill and I joined the Friday restaurant group. Sitting at tables for four or six with other operators, we were able to visit with some of the old-timers and learn a lot about how our header department interacted with other departments and plants in the G.E. complex.

The more Bill and I visited with each other, the more we found we had in common—similar career objectives and similar family situations. Bill's mother had passed away when he was a boy, and I had lost my father. Bill's father and sisters stayed together and helped each other, as did my mother, sisters, and brother.

We both had a strong desire to go to college and study electrical engineering, and we both lacked the money to do that. At that time—the beginning of our careers—we were focused on doing well at our jobs and earning as much as possible for college.

During lunch one day, Bill told me about his boat. It was an old captain's gig hull, retired from the Navy, about twenty-eight feet long, with a cabin, but no engine when he bought it. He had it moored at a pier in the Saugus River at East Saugus. He had been working on the boat for some months; he'd found a used Dodge automobile engine that would fit the hull and was in the process of installing it. I offered to give him a hand when I had time on the weekends. I found working on the boat relaxing. Bill concentrated on the mechanical work, and I did the electrical.

Our objective was to get the boat running before the fall storms set in, so we could take it out in Boston harbor and do some fishing. We had to replace all of the wiring, lights, bilge pump, and controls. By working a few extra nights, we completed the work and judged the boat seaworthy. Now we were ready for a test cruise. We carefully stowed life vests, a life preserver, and a bailing bucket—just in case.

The first day of fishing outside Boston harbor was worth all the work we had put into the boat. Bill was pilot and paid for the gas; I furnished the sandwiches and beer. We caught a few haddock and some cod. Best of all, we had the day to talk about our career dreams and plans for the future.

I told Bill about my conversation with my Uncle Bill in New Jersey the previous year. Uncle Bill had advised me: "Find a steady job, adopt an interested attitude and aggressive work style, always act as if you have an ownership interest in the company. The objective is to attract the attention of management and to let them know you're determined to advance and improve your status. And, while on the job, stay busy, help others, ask questions, and have a good attitude. This work ethic, followed consistently while you're young, along with night school courses, is my formula for your success."

I had already enrolled for the fall term in engineering classes three nights a week at Franklin Union Technical Institute. We kicked around Uncle Bill's wisdom at some length during the day, particularly his parting words: "Don't let anything interfere with your night classes or your work ethic and you will succeed."

Sadly, I never saw Uncle Bill again, but his advice was etched solidly in my mind, and is as real today as if our conversation was yesterday.

Regarding night classes, Bill Wild said he had given some thought to night study, but had lots of questions about cost, subjects, schedules, and so forth. I was able to answer most of them.

We gradually came up with a plan of action. First, Bill would enroll at Franklin Union. We could ride to classes together and discuss our subjects together. Together, we would gain a lot more from our studies than if we went at them separately.

Second, we would take Uncle Bill's advice and be eager workers at our jobs at General Electric. We would let supervisors know we were qualified and eager to advance in position and salary. We would also check out the opportunities in the apprentice program at General Electric, or the possibility of transfer to jobs in their engineering department.

Yes, we would definitely work together as a team to achieve our career goals. Bill's ultimate career goal was to work up to top management in a large corporation where he would have some assurance of adequate income and a comfortable retirement. My ultimate career goal was more nebulous, but it did include building my own company and doing something electrical. We would carefully plan our work and work our plan. We sealed our "career team" pact with a solemn handshake.

B ill and I worked together as a highly successful team for eleven years. We credited our early success to our mutual vow to allow nothing to interfere with our night school studies, and to our eagerness to advance in position and salary at work.

We made it a point to have lunch together every work day when possible. We each knew that the other Bill was always available to discuss problems, to help or advise, to relax or discuss whatever our day-to-day experiences brought.

Meanwhile, back at the header department, my battery of four headers were up and running in two weeks, mainly owing to a lot of help from Mr. Allen and other operators. Also, the boss made it a point to give me some of the less complicated bolt orders to produce, which may have accounted for the fact that my headers were already producing as many bolts as those of the average operator.

Bill and I started our "super employee" program the week after our fishing trip. We both arrived at our headers every morning fifteen minutes early, in time to get all our supplies ready and to make any mechanical adjustments necessary. When the clock hit 8:00, we turned on our machines. Then at quitting time, 5:00 P.M., we stayed long enough to clean up our headers until they shone, and to turn in any production of the day.

Part of our "super employee" program was looking for opportunities to visit with the other operators and ask about their career plans, to talk with other employees in other departments about their jobs and future prospects, and to look seriously into the GE apprentice program. Some of our questions came up at a Friday lunch at our favorite restaurant as we shared a table with four of the older header operators. We asked them about their jobs and how to get ahead.

"Well, I'll tell ya, when I landed my job as a young guy, the department was fairly new, and the operator job paid better than most because the noise and accident risk were greater than most," one of the guys said.

"Did you want to change jobs after a year or two?" I asked.

"Yes, because of fear of going deaf, mainly," another man said.

"Why didn't you move on?" Bill asked.

The first man gave Bill a serious look, shaking his head, and replied, "Because all four of us had families to support, with kids and all. We could not make enough money to put away very much, and changing jobs would mean a big cut in take-home pay. The longer you stay, the rougher it is to change jobs. Also, when the demand for bolts goes down, as it does every three or four years, you face a layoff of a month or two and there go your savings."

So much for a career as a machine operator. For many guys, this would be pretty good work and pretty good pay. The job did have its drawbacks though, as most jobs do. Bill and I appreciated the fact that at that point, we had operator's jobs, and a base to start working from.

When all our headers were banging away on long runs, Bill and I would be tempted to goof off a little bit. The operators, when setting up a header, had to concentrate for long periods, peering down into the header making various adjustments, and most guys got quite tense in the process. This was a good time for Bill to pin an insulting sign on a guy's back for him to wear around all day, or to paint his heels with the white lead we used as wire lubricant.

Every now and then an official would bring a tour group through the department—sometimes six or eight guys in the apprentice program, or sometimes a group of G.E. executives. They all seemed to be fascinated by the stream of bolts flying out of our headers. The operators, every few minutes, would reach down and grab one of the bolts, smoking hot as it left the header, rub it around in their palms briefly, then examine and measure it. Often a visitor would ask in gestures whether it was okay for him to look at one, and he would get a nod from the operator. He would grab the smoking bolt from the header as he saw us doing, and it would usually end up between his fingers. For the next five minutes he would dance around holding onto his burned hand, to the accompaniment of hidden snickering from the operators. (They, of course, were careful to touch the hot bolts only with their work-hardened palms, not between their fingers.)

We had a very impressive-looking machine located near my headers, across the aisle and behind Mr. Allen's desk. It was an automatic surface grinder with a magnetic table. The operator would place a piece of steel, like one of our header dies (about two inches in diameter and two inches long) on the steel table, and adjust the grinding wheel above the die just barely touching the top surface of the die, then turn the machine on. The table, having a very strong magnetic field, held the die securely in place while the grinding wheel automatically passed back and forth across the top of the die, taking about 1/1000 inch of steel off on each pass, or whatever it was set to take off.

Visitors were always attracted to this state-of-the-art machine by the great stream of sparks it put out. Often, when I saw a group coming up the floor past Bill's headers, I would place a die on the surface grinder and turn it on just before the group arrived at my headers. Invariably, someone would rush over to peer at the automatic grinder. And invariably, one of the viewers would have steel buttons in the fly of his trousers, common in those days. The strong magnetic field would grab the guy's fly area and pull him in against the table, holding him there terrified until I came to his rescue. All the operators convulsed in laughter.

None of these jokes was perpetrated when Mr. Allen or Mr. Hooper was in the department. However, a few laughs broke the monotony and tension of keeping the headers operating. I guess my progress was okay, because I received several compliments from Mr. Allen, and even Mr. Hooper would come by now and then, smiling and dispensing pats on the back.

In addition to learning how to become header machine operators, Bill and I learned a great deal about machine shop practices, including the proper set-up and operation of lathes, drill presses, punch presses, and other equipment. We also became familiar with metal plating procedures, screw machine operation, and metal threading equipment. It was part of our "super employee" program to learn all we could about the overall shop operations.

At the going-away party for a schoolmate leaving for the Army, there were one hundred or more at the dinner, and most stayed on for beer and gossip. Soon after dinner some guys began to sing popular songs in small groups here and there around the room. Bill and I started singing together for the first time. Bill had a fine tenor voice and a talent for harmonizing, And I sang the lead. It was fun and sounded pretty good to us, and I guess to the others, because they kept us singing until close to midnight. We had to leave then to pick up Bill's dad at a party he was attending with a group of G.E. people.

That night we were using Bill's dad's car because my beat-up old Chevy was in need of some engine work. We picked up Mr. Wild and drove to their home in Saugus. He asked us to come in and talk for a bit.

We sat at the kitchen table and talked for an hour or two. Bill's dad was interested in our plans, our goals, and the subjects we were studying at night school. He had heard very good reports about our work in the header department.

We told him all about our career team, our "earn while you learn" program, and our determination to become electrical engineers. Mr. Wild was all for our career program, telling us to stick with it, to study at night and work hard in the days. I remember him saying, "Smart dogs take the rugged trails, puppies take the highway."

Our night class program worked out quite well. Since we had committed to the school and to each other for three nights a week, we never considered cutting class. School took top priority— one of the benefits of our partnership program.

After work and a bite to eat, we would drive into Boston and attend classes. On the way home, we would review what was discussed in class. We had homework after every class, and here again, we discussed the homework before the next class. Frequently, if one of us had trouble understanding something covered in the text or lecture, the other would come up with an explanation. We often discussed school subjects during lunch breaks at work, too.

We took our program seriously and made night courses a part of our lives for the following three years. This is not to say that our "earning while learning" program was any substitute for a college education, but it worked wonders for us, lacking the money for college. This routine of our adopted work ethic in our jobs, combined with night study, established a lifestyle which steered us away from the usual pitfalls encountered by some of our peers who lacked a game plan for their future.

In the fall of 1935, General Electric started withholding a few dollars of our pay for the new federal Social Security program. This was supposed to supplement our retirement when the time came.

G.E. had an employee union, independent from any national union, and we were not required to pay dues. The pay scale seemed to be fair, and working conditions were good, except for the noisy header machines that kept our ears ringing all night long. We could not wear earplugs because they might prevent us from hearing sounds of trouble if one of our headers started to break up.

The noisy header machines were a major concern to my mother. We had several serious discussions about the danger of the noise. She pointed out that the human ear is not constructed to withstand such unnatural noise indefinitely, and it would result in gradual loss of hearing. I promised Mother I would operate headers only as long as it took to find a job in the electrical field.

Even though we had steady jobs with fair pay at G.E. and had learned a lot about machine shop operations, we were mentally prepared to change to any job offering new experience important to our careers.

In mid-1936 Bill and I were using Mr. Wild's car on a Saturday night, when we stopped by about midnight to pick up Bill's dad at a friend's house. When we arrived at Bill's house, Mr. Wild asked us to come in for a short talk. The conversation went on for an hour around the kitchen table.

Mr. Wild had had a conversation with someone he called Whitey, who said he would sponsor Bill and me as engineering students in the electrical department of Bethlehem Steel Shipbuilding Division at Quincy, Massachusetts, if we were interested. Apparently the fact that we were attending night classes, and doing quite well, qualified us as engineering students.

Mr. Wild understood from his conversation that Bethlehem was beginning to beef up the work force at the shipyard in preparation for expected Navy and Maritime Commission contracts. We talked it over, including the fact we could see very little opportunity for an engineering career at G.E. We expected the pay scale would be higher than at G.E., but we had no clue as to just what we would be doing in the Bethlehem electrical department. The offer seemed to us to be the route to better jobs—certainly a chance for something better than continuing as header machine operators. We agreed to change jobs to shipbuilding, if offered.

Word came back in a few days through Whitey and Mr. Wild that we now had jobs at Bethlehem's Fore River shipyard, and were to report to their employment office at Quincy, Massachusetts, within two weeks. The next Monday Bill and I gave notice at G.E. that Friday would be our last day.

"Hey, I can't believe it. Why are you guys leaving? Can I do anything to change your mind?" Mr. Allen asked.

Both of us answered pretty much the same: we appreciated all that G.E. had done for us. We enjoyed working there, but we both wanted an electrical career and we had an opportunity with Bethlehem's electrical department.

Friday lunch at our favorite restaurant on Lynn Common was quite an event. Many of the header machine operators were there, wishing the two Bills from Saugus luck, buying our lunch. Some said they envied our determination to build a career.

"If it turns out you guys don't like buildin' ships, you can always get a job as header operators," one old-timer said.

Back in the header department we collected our personal things, said goodbye to our friends, and went over to Mr. Hooper's office for our final pay.

Mr. Hooper was obviously upset.

"I can't believe you're making such a foolhardy change, and after all we've done for you. People who build ships are drifters, criminals, murderers, drunks, who can't hold down jobs. You'll both be out on the streets within six months, and back in this office on your knees begging for your jobs back," he said.

We thanked him for all he and other people in the department had done for us, and then we left. He did get a little carried away, but we understood all his fuss was a bit of a compliment to us, and that he really did not want to see us leave. We walked out through the great iron gate for the last time with no regrets, looking forward to a new career adventure.

Once again, someone had recommended us to our new employer based on reports of our work ethic, night study program, and long-term goals. The fact that the word did get around about our determination to advance encouraged us to continue our "career team" program.

3

Shipbuilding with Bethlehem Steel

B efore giving our notice to General Electric, Bill and I did a lot of talking, reading, and thinking about working in a shipyard. We knew Mr. Hooper was overstating the facts when he warned us about all the characters who built ships. My Uncle Bill, whom I had visited the year before in New Jersey, had spent years as an employee in the Philadelphia Navy Yard, and he had nothing but positive things to say about shipyard work. On the other hand, we knew that all construction work has some danger involved, and that some employees would have prison records. Also, by its very nature, it was not steady work.

After the end of the ship construction program associated with the World War, commercial and naval shipbuilding had slowed down. Private shipyards had little work, and so their skilled specialists, after completing a ship under construction in Boston, for example, often traveled to other East Coast or West Coast shipyards looking for work in their specialty. This made some people think that these specialists were "drifters."

There were some very good reasons for a person to consider working in a shipyard, particularly if contemplating a career in any of the crafts associated with building or construction. The design of merchant and naval ships had progressed to a point where the very latest technological developments in most crafts were employed. Modern merchant ships and naval combat ships were virtual seagoing cities as far as their facilities are concerned. Vessels were designed to carry fuel sufficient for weeks of propulsion, as well as for generation of electric power for heat, lighting, cooking, and power auxiliaries. A big ship had a sewage treatment system, a telephone system, fire prevention and control equipment, doctors and hospital facilities, worldwide communication and navigation facilities, maintenance and repair facilities for all installed equipment, and countless other detailed needs. And all these systems were designed to function while the vessel was rolling and pitching through stormy seas, and in wide variations of temperature, humidity, and vibration.

Any person interested in a technological industry could gain experience in a wide spectrum of equipment installation, testing, and troubleshooting, and in equipment ranging from electric motors and motor control equipment to various types of lighting and control, power switchboards, computers of various types, and so on. There was no place like a shipyard to check it all out. On the down side, it did get freezing cold working in shipbuilding during northern winters.

The thought of becoming involved in a giant maze of the very latest in electrical equipment was very exciting to Bill and me. To be sure that we would find our way to the shipyard on time Monday morning, we made a trial run from Saugus to Quincy on Saturday.

We left Saugus bright and early on Monday, driving through heavy traffic jams in downtown Boston and on to the shipyard at Quincy. Thanks to our test run on Saturday, we were able to arrive at the shipyard, find a parking space, and walk into the personnel office well before opening time. Our travel time was about one and one-half hours.

We signed in on the registration form at the personnel counter and sat down to wait our call. The crowd of men in the office was apparently doing the Depression routine of signing in and hoping for a call for work.

After a while our names were called. The nervous wait was over. We left the crowd and were escorted into an office where we were given personnel forms to fill out. The magic phrase that set us apart from the crowd of job applicants was "engineering student." We had no idea whether our program at Franklin Union was in any way helpful in receiving the job offer, or if it was instead contacts on our behalf by Bill's dad's friend. Whatever did it, we were grateful and determined to make a go of it. We would continue our eager-employee work ethic and career team program.

There were no pre-employment interviews or aptitude tests at Bethlehem. Instead, we were escorted through the shipyard to the electric shop in an older utility building. We climbed the stairs to the second floor and were shown a long workbench. We could store our lunches and personal things on the far end of the bench. A row of windows behind the bench overlooked the shipyard, but they were covered with grime inside and out, and all that could be seen through them was a faint daylight glow.

After we were introduced all around to the dozen or so other shop employees, the foreman showed us our workstations. Bill and I were to work side by side at the workbench. At each position there was an arbor press installed on the bench along with a stack of steel rods of various diameters, each about six inches long. The arbor presses were set up to manufacture shipboard cable straps, or "hangers."

Bill and I lost no time in getting our eager employee routine under way. We made it a point to get acquainted with all the shop employees and every electrician we came in contact with from the ship. At the same time, we soon were putting out a lot more work than most of the others. Also, we kept our work areas organized and clean. I bugged the foreman until he gave me a brochure detailing each type of shipboard cable, per U.S. Navy, Bureau of Ships standards.

Although making cable hangers was obviously an easy job for beginners in the department, we found the electric shop to be a very important part of electrical work aboard ship. Practically every piece of electrical equipment installed aboard ship had to first be routed through the electric shop to have stuffing tubes installed. The stuffing tube was designed for an electric cable to enter a piece of equipment through the protective equipment case, and to maintain the watertight integrity of the equipment.

To install the stuffing tube, the equipment case had to be drilled and tapped (a hole drilled and threaded), often requiring disassembly of the equipment. Bill was really interested in this part of the electric shop's work, learning who did what and why. My interest was in the electrical installations aboard ship, and in what goes on in an engineering department. We were quite sure we would graduate from hanger making before too long, and we kept our eager employee work ethic going every day.

After a week or two working at Bethlehem Steel, driving from our Saugus homes through Boston every morning, then stopping at Franklin Union three nights a week for evening classes on the way home, we began to talk about leaving home and finding an apartment closer to the shipyard. We spent a Saturday looking and found one on the second floor of a fine old colonial-style house in a nice area of Wallaston, just a few miles north of Quincy on the highway to Boston. The pleasant old gentleman who owned the house lived with his wife on the ground floor. The apartment consisted of two bedrooms, a bath, a small living room, and a kitchen. It was furnished, even with pots and pans. We made a deal at a reasonable price and moved some of our things from home the next day.

The apartment worked out great. There was more time for study, plus more sleep in the morning. We made a deal first thing after moving in: we would take turns cooking on a weekly basis. On the weeks I was to cook, Bill would wash dishes and vacuum; the next week, vice versa. We made lunches to carry to work. For dinner Bill was strong on fried potatoes and hamburger patties. I hit the spaghetti route pretty heavy. After work on Fridays, we headed for Saugus with our books and soiled laundry. The apartment was fun for us, and it proved to be a major saving in money and travel time—another plus for our career team program.

After our second week of making cable hangers, a man came into the shop looking for me. He introduced himself as Roland

Avery. He was a stout, good-natured fellow about thirty-five years old, dressed in the usual electrician's brown coveralls and white cap.

"You'll be working with me on the ships starting tomorrow morning," he said.

"Great! What will we be doing?" I asked.

"We'll be installing mechanical signaling equipment on four freighters under construction. You can leave your personal stuff here."

The next morning Roland came by and took me on a tour of the shipyard. Ships were being built on ways resembling giant railroad tracks, except that each track was about two feet wide and the two tracks were perhaps twenty feet apart. The tracks were sloped at a slight angle as they extended about one thousand feet across the yard and into the Fore River. Keel blocks, where the keel of the vessel was to be placed at the very start of construction, were located exactly between the two tracks for most of the thousand feet.

We stood by a rack holding large formed steel plates. Each plate had strange marks painted on it; these indicated exactly where the plate was to be installed on the freighter in our view, under construction on the ways.

On either side of the ways was a paved area with a set of tracks running the full length of the ways. Huge whirly cranes moved back and forth on the tracks, their hook loads of structural steel or equipment poised above the hull under construction.

Alongside the ways on the pavement was a maze of pipes, hoses, electric cables, oxygen and acetylene tanks, and welding machines. Staging surrounded the hull on both sides. A gangway stretched from the pier to the main deck area of the hull, and hundreds of cables, pipes, and hoses stretched up the side of the hull to the main deck area. There was so much to see, understand, and absorb, with the help of Roland's expert observations.

Roland identified the largest hull on the ways that day, an aircraft carrier, by a Bethlehem job number; she was later to be christened USS *Wasp* CV-7. "She was started as a battle cruiser to counter the German pocket battleships that were raising hell with the British merchant fleet in the early days of the war. However, after British aircraft proved able to handle the German naval threat, work was stopped on the battle cruiser hull and it was redesigned an aircraft carrier. There's not much the crew can do waiting for design changes, so we call it the old man's home," he said.

Roland explained that the hulls stayed on the building ways only until all basic hull structural work was finished, propellor shafts in place, and compartments tested. Then the hull was fitted with a series of cradle-like devices and wood blocks which rested on the launching ways. The ways were covered with heavy, thick grease. At exactly the right moment, after the hull had been chris- tened in the launching ceremony, she slid down the ways stern first and into the river. Although the hull is given a name during the launching ceremony, the shipyard continues to identify the vessel by the hull number.

There were two freighters at the outfitting dock. Roland said these were the two ships we would be working on. One was the American Export Lines SS *Explorer*, and the other the Panama Railway Company's SS *Ancon*.

The dock was a beehive of activity, with men rushing back and forth, tractors pulling trailers full of equipment, the gangway crowded with workers moving to and from the ship. Welding machines on the ship filled the air with a high-pitched whine, and chipping hammers added to the racket aboard ship.

"Say, Roland, if the work we're about to do is mechanical, how come it's in the electrical department?" I asked.

"Because the company considers it a signal system," he replied.

A heavyset man in his fifties joined us at the gangway. Roland introduced him as an electrical supervisor.

"Where have you been working before this?" he said to me.

"I've been with General Electric,"I replied.

His eyes opened wide. He looked me all over, and with a big smile said, "Great, we can sure use you! Welcome aboard!"

At that time, the maritime industry insisted on a foolproof mechanical signaling system between the navigating bridge and the engine room, so that when the bridge officer signaled the engine room to move the ship forward or astern, the man on watch in the engine room could immediately acknowledge the command. Likewise, when it became necessary to sound the ship's whistle, it simply must work. Apparently, there was no confidence at that time in electrical signal systems.

The engine order telegraph instrument was located near the ship's wheel in the pilot house. It was a waist-high brass pedestal with a rounded top and vertical operating handles. Solid brass wires ran between the instrument in the pilot house to a similar instrument in the engine room. The system for operating the ship's whistle also used solid brass wire between whistle levers on the bridge and the whistle, which was located forward of the smoke stack.

The brass wires were used only to mechanically transfer the motion of the handle of the instrument on the bridge to the instrument in the engine and vice versa; no electrical function was involved.

The installation of these mechanical systems was a very fussy job. The route that the operating wire took had to be in a straight line wherever possible, using chains around pulleys to change direction. However, once installed and adjusted properly, the system worked well.

Roland had the first hull pretty well under way, and the second about half finished, when he turned the job over to me. He made it a point to stop by and check on me every morning, and was very supportive in making sure I had all necessary tools and material to do the work. When Roland left, my boss was the man in charge over all ship construction.

As my mechanical signal system installation job progressed, it was often necessary for me to stop my work to wait for some other craftsmen to finish their work, like installing another bulkhead or rerouting a big pipe that was in my way. During these delays, I would visit with the electricians at their jobs. I would ask to see layout drawings, wiring diagrams, and the interiors of panels being hooked up. The electricians were all quite friendly and seemed happy to answer my questions about their work. Most had spent four years as apprentices before training for shipboard work. The electricians were easy to spot among the workers: they all wore brown coveralls and white, usually dirty, caps.

When working in spaces with other crafts, I always tried to be friendly and helpful to others, including low-rated helpers. Work attitude was most important. Everyone knew I was determined to get ahead.

The common complaint among electricians was the difficulty in arranging for service crafts to do welding, hole drilling, chipping, and other support jobs. I realized that there was little I could do in my installations without the assistance of service crafts. If I wanted to mount something on a bulkhead (that is, a wall), I needed a welder. To drill a hole through a girder, I needed a driller. Sometimes a burner with his acetylene torch was needed, or a chipper with his pneumatic chisel. And usually everyone else needed them, too. My solution was to get to know these people, to help them move their gear into my space, and to compliment them on a job well done. It really made a difference in the volume of work I was able to finish.

At home on weekends, friends thinking about applying for a job in a shipyard would ask me about what it was like and how dangerous it was. "Ship construction probably is more dangerous than building work, but once aboard ship you can see most hazards and tend to be much more alert than usual," I would say.

"You watch where you're walking and what's going on overhead. You don't look at arc welding, and you check out adequate ventilation below deck. Also, there's some new language to learn—it's 'forward and aft,' not 'front and back.' You go 'below,' not 'downstairs,' and stairs are called 'ladders.' The floor is called the 'deck,' walls are called 'bulkheads,' and ceilings are called 'overhead.' However, before long, you learn the lingo."

Bill and I were having lunch in the shop one day when Pete Debes, a man Bill had told me about, came by. He was a tall, husky fellow in his mid-thirties, pleasantly gruff and friendly. Pete was in charge of all electrical work on some of the ships under construction. I had questions to ask, mostly about engine room equipment. Pete patiently explained the various functions, told me how it all went together, and encouraged me to learn more about the main generators and main switchboard.

When construction reached a point where I could go no further in my job, I asked the electrical supervisor Roland had introduced me to (on that first day boarding ship) if I could get involved in some fill-in electrical work.

"Hey, you bet. I'll get you a contract to install lighting panels, cable, and fixtures," he said.

He furnished drawings, all the materials needed, and an installation contract for the number of hours to complete the job. If I completed it in less time, I would receive a bonus.

After my conversation with the supervisor, I was elated to be considered a journeyman electrician—a title others had to work four years as an apprentice to achieve. Why, after a few months, was I now an electrician? I thought back to when Roland introduced me to the supervisor, and his surprise and delight when I said I had been with General Electric. Maybe he thought I was an engineer for G.E.?

No one had to show me what to do, because I had studied every phase of electrical work on ships for weeks. It helped to know many of the supporting craftspeople. It also helped, when I needed something from the electric shop, to have the support of Bill, who made sure I had super service. The big boss, Pete Debes, came by frequently to check progress on my first electrical job. I really enjoyed the work. My first contract was finished and closed out well ahead of the specified time. More contracts followed, and I split my time between electrical work and mechanical signal work. Within the first six months at Bethlehem, I had advanced to journeyman electrician. The work and the pay were great!

Soon the first of the three freighters on which I had installed the mechanical signal system was ready for dock trials. Everything worked fine, and with steam finally up to pressure in the boilers, we could test the ship's whistle. It sounded loud and clear.

Builders' trials were next on the schedule. This was when a select crew of builders' employees took the ship out to sea for a day, to show representatives of the purchaser that the vessel handled properly and that the propulsion system fuel economy was within contract limits. Tests included various speeds forward and astern, and they also showed that the anchor machinery worked.

My name appeared on the list of builders' trial personnel. I manned a station in the engine room at a telephone connected to the bridge, to report problems or operating information. The trip was interesting. Time flew by, and soon we were heading back to the shipyard after dark, sporting a household broom attached high on the mast in the rigging. This was an old custom to let the world know the vessel passed all tests—a clean sweep.

After our day of cruising around in the Atlantic Ocean on builders' trials, seated at a comfortable spot in the engine room listening to the hum of the generators and the steady drone of other equipment, my first day back in construction was pretty noisy. Riveters, chippers, and hammering all contributed to the din. However, about three minutes before end of shift it became eerily quiet all over the ship. Then the whistle sounded, and a wall of men erupted from every hatch and doorway, running at full speed toward the only gangway leading to the dock. The first man to reach the dock had bragging rights for a day.

There was a lot of good-natured teasing and dirty tricks going on during construction between workers in different crafts. Working closely together in restricted spaces, often competing for space to install equipment, led to testy situations.

One dirty trick was to weld a man's lunch box to the deck when the man was out of the area. Then when the quitting time whistle blew, and the guy dashed on deck to grab his lunch box on the run, he ended up flying through space.

The USS *Wasp* was just a hull number when Bill and I started work at the shipyard, but activity picked up soon after as revised drawings were completed, changing the battle cruiser into an aircraft carrier. Progress was apparent: the hull was painted, the massive launching cradles were installed, and a date was set for the launching. It was a big deal for the government and for the company both when a Navy ship was to be launched. The government chose some notable woman or the wife of an important official to do the christening. She stood on a platform high up against the bunting-draped bow, and just before the vessel was to start moving down the ways, she was to break the bottle of champagne against the bow, saying, "I christen you the USS *Wasp*."

When the day came for launching, I was assigned a telephone job with the launching crew. I was stationed down on the ways, beneath the hull and near the stern. By that time, the weight of the hull had been transferred from the keel blocks to the greased launching ways. (A ship is launched stern first.)

The hull was held in place on the ways and prevented from moving by heavy steel plates, anchoring it in place. Burners, with their torches flaring, stood ready at each of the anchor plates, ready to start burning them loose in a predetermined sequence, once the word was given, coordinated by those of us on the telephones.

A large crowd had gathered in the roped-off area around the bow staging. Speeches were made, and there was applause now and then. A flight of six Navy biplanes appeared overhead, flying in "V" formation. They buzzed the *Wasp* as she slid down the ways. In the process of turning back toward their base, two of the planes collided and crashed, killing the crews. The tragedy placed a damper on everyone at the launching that day.

An old shipwright near me shook his head and said, "She's a blood ship now. To have a death at a launching means she will always have bad luck."

Over a year had passed in our jobs with Bethlehem Steel. Both Bill and I continued our approach of working hard, taking night classes, and getting acquainted with lots of people. On the ships, I had advanced to full electrician status, doing all kinds of wiring jobs. The night classes were paying off with our knowledge of the latest developments in electrical equipment, control wiring for motor controllers, and so forth. Bill and I were able to help some of our older co-workers understand the new electrical symbols and circuitry. We were journeymen electricians, often doing lead work. Bill had advanced to electrician status in the electric shop—exactly the kind of work he had hoped to be assigned.

One day the big boss, Pete Debes, stopped by the electric shop and told Bill he would like to pick us up at our apartment the next morning. He wanted to talk to us in his office and would give us a ride home after work. We had classes that evening, but we were in no mood to discuss electrical theory. Pete had given Bill no hint as to what was up.

The next morning we watched as Pete pulled up to the curb by our apartment in his big Nash sedan. He drove us to his private parking space at the shipyard. He told us to meet him there at 5:15 P.M. for a ride home, and then we went on to his office.

"It's the Union Iron Works in San Francisco that I want to talk to you about," Pete said. "There's rumors around that we're reactivating the yard. It's been in mothballs since the war. Actually, the yard is partially in operation doing ship repair work. The company has a contract to build two McCall class destroyers."

He showed us a drawing of the Navy's newest class of destroyer, a single-stack, streamlined, high-speed vessel. Aluminum was substituted for steel in much of the superstructure—a new design feature.

"I've received orders to transfer to the Union Iron Works, and to prepare for the construction of the destroyers," Pete said. "I'd like to transfer you two Bills to work with me, along with Harry Stone, an ex-Navy man.

"You three would form the nucleus of my crew. Bill Wild would set up and run the electric shop. Bill Bright would work with engineering on drawings for construction of power and lighting systems aboard ship, plus maintenance and other details. Harry Stone would prepare for his specialties, interior communication and gunfire control systems.

"Bethlehem would pay for your transportation to San Francisco. You could travel by automobile, train or bus. Bill Wild and Harry Stone would leave within a week. Bill Bright would follow when his work in process was finished, probably in two to three weeks.

"I want you to kick it around together. This would be a big step for you to take, but I would like to have your answer as soon as possible," Pete said.

We walked back to the electric shop in a state of mild confusion. This was a large electrical department, full of older men who had years more seniority than we. Were we chosen because we were students, single, working well together as a team? Probably, but this would mean a major promotion for both of us, from electricians to electrical supervisors.

Going west sounded like high adventure. We could make school arrangements in San Francisco. There was now no doubt we had attracted the attention of management with our management-friendly work ethic, as we had at General Electric. Within half an hour we were back at Pete's office. We thanked him for the opportunity and assured him we would not let him down.

The news spread quickly around the shipyard. A rumor about reactivating Union Iron Works was now confirmed as fact. On the way back to the electric shop, we were stopped several times to answer questions about why we were chosen. It was no secret that Bill and I were in the shipyard to work, to learn, and to advance. At that time, our attitude was unusual among employees, so we drew the attention of management. Our career goals, though, remained nebulous. Bill continued to dream of advancement to top management in a large corporation, and my dream involved building my own electrical manufacturing company.

Harry Stone joined us later that day. Harry was about six feet tall and thirty-five years old. He had a happy, relaxed disposition, and his steady smile flashed the gold crowns on two upper front teeth. Besides his Navy shipboard electrical experience, Harry had worked in the Bath Iron Works shipyard in Maine. Harry and Bill decided they would buy a car and drive to San Francisco, sharing the cost of the car. They would find a place to live, and save me a room. I would wind up our affairs at Franklin Union and the apartment, and join them in three to four weeks.

About two weeks later, Bill wrote, saying the drive had taken only five days. They found nice clean rooms over a restaurant on Bayshore Boulevard, two miles south of downtown and ten minutes from the shipyard.

My work was wound up in three weeks, with lots of help from the crew. In answer to their questions about why Bill and I were chosen, I told everyone that I had no idea who might have recommended us, and the best source for answers would probably be our boss, Pete Debes.

The last day at Fore River finally came. My priority was to get under way to San Francisco. I cleaned up the apartment, settled with the owner, and moved my things back home to Saugus.

My focus continued to be on my career goal—someday to build my own company, but for the next few years to earn and learn everything possible for success.

4

Shipbuilding in San Francisco

I had to decide how to travel to San Francisco—by rail, car or bus. Driving alone across country in my old, beat-up Chevy was not for me. I chose the bus in order to see more of the country.

I left home on a Sunday morning with all the belongings I could carry in one suitcase, and boarded a Greyhound bus in Boston. My ticket routed me through New York City to Chicago, St. Louis, Oklahoma City, Dallas, El Paso, Tucson, Los Angeles, and finally San Francisco.

That Greyhound bus proved to be a winner. My seat partners were often familiar with the countryside we were passing through and served as expert guides. The bus stopped every two hours or so for rest and exercise, and the meal stops were at good restaurants. Bus transfers in major cities gave a person an opportunity to explore the city for an hour or two.

Bill and Harry met me at the San Francisco bus terminal. We drove south on Bayshore Boulevard to a restaurant with big lettering across the front: "Rosy's Good Eats." Above it was our apartment. Bill and I shared a large room on the second floor with beds and closets at each end. It was nicely furnished and had bay windows that swung open over busy Bayshore Boulevard.

Next I was introduced to Rosy, a jolly woman in her fifties. Rosy's brother also lived there and did odd jobs; the guys called him "Hammerhead." Another roomer, about ten years older than I and quite a bit shorter, was Dave Williams, who worked a few blocks away. Bill had named him "the Nipper."

Rosy's cook would make brown-bag lunches for the three of us every work day, and serve us breakfast and dinner. If we wanted something special, the cook would prepare it for us, provided we gave him the ingredients beforehand; we felt at home with Boston specialties such as corned beef and cabbage, or good old-fashioned baked beans.

The Union Iron Works shipyard had been reactivated after being shut down for several years. Building ways were in place, with hull construction under way. Bill had taken over the electric shop and was busy preparing to handle the expected heavy workload. It would be some weeks before the hulls would be ready for electricians, so my job was to keep current with progress in the engineering department for construction drawings, and to be available if needed for ship repair activity.

In addition to Union Iron Works, at that time Bethlehem also owned the Hunter's Point dry-dock, the largest on the West Coast. Some ships would come in for repair at Hunter's Point, and others would tie up along the docks in San Francisco. A long dock was under construction at Union Iron Works for ship repair and outfitting. I was to oversee electrical crews working in any of these areas.

Suddenly, my job was no longer working with tools, but planning, organizing, and supervising electrical work. That suited me just fine, and Bill liked his new position in charge of the electric shop. Our career teamwork, our work plan, and night engineering study program had produced firm results much earlier than we expected. We were electrical supervisors less than three years after graduating from high school.

Of course, we were also presented with continuing challenges. Everyone in the shipyard seemed to know that the two Bills from Boston (as they all called us because we "talked funny") were chosen from others at Bethlehem's main shipyard, so we must know just about everything there was to know about the electrical part of shipbuilding. The challenge was not so much to do what we had been trained to do and had learned from job experience, but to confidently take on unusual or new projects that would come along from time to time.

Soon the long outfitting pier was finished, and we started to get very interesting ship repair jobs. One was a Matson luxury liner, in for its annual overhaul and the installation of gravity-type lifeboat davits—new at that time. We also did the overhaul of a U.S. Army Corps of Engineers dredge. A parade of many types and sizes of vessels followed—many with outmoded direct current electrical systems, and some World War I era equipment.

This repair work was a challenge for Bill and me, resulting in much research activity to find the answers to problems that would come up. Bill really liked ship repair activity—the ongoing challenge of updating old systems and equipment. My preference was new construction, but we did our best at whatever job came along.

Before leaving Boston, I advised Franklin Union Technical Institute that Bill and I would be gone for a year or two and asked if they could suggest a correspondence course that would keep us up to speed until we returned. As a result, we began receiving material soon after I arrived in San Francisco. Our study program kept us hitting the books in our rooms, each evening Sunday through Thursday. Friday night was our night on the town.

After a few months of living at Rosy's, Harry did some investigation of the house rental market. He was convinced that the four of us could rent a house and hire a housekeeper for a lot less money than we paid for room and board at Rosy's. He found a nice home on Stanyon Street, just a few blocks from Golden Gate Park. Typical of downtown San Francisco, it was on a hilly street with no space between houses. The garage was at street level, the house extended two stories above, and it was completely furnished. The employment agency would provide a live-in housekeeper. Total cost, including utilities, food and rent, would be much less for all of us than living at Rosy's. We gave Rosy two weeks notice and moved into the Stanyon Street house.

Harry hired a pleasant woman named Lillian to do the cooking, lunches and housework. Lillian proved to be a good housekeeper. Her cooking would not win any prizes, but it was not too bad. However, she was not used to our oven, and charred the south end of our Thanksgiving turkey, leaving just breast meat and wings to dine on.

As the first destroyer hull began taking shape, our crews started building up pretty fast. We welcomed two more men from Fore River shipyard who had electrical experience, Oliver "Mac" Mageehon and Ernie Bernhagen. These two men were outstanding workers and became close friends, too. Ernie specialized in lighting systems, and Mac, trained as an engineer, in interior communications systems.

As the crews started to build, with many strangers working in tight spaces aboard ship, we gave a lot of thought to how we could get the crew better acquainted, and to work together better. The answer came to us rather suddenly.

Friday was payday. Supervisors were given paychecks for their crews before noon, and distributed them during the day. At some point the crew began betting on the last five numbers of the serial number on their checks—as to who would have the best "poker hand." The betting spread from the electrical crew to other crafts.

Management prohibited betting on the job, but that didn't stop it. Each man in the crew would give a bet—say five dollars—to a designated cashier in the crew on Friday morning. Then after work on Friday night, they would all troop into the Illinois Tavern, two blocks from the main gate, to compare check numbers. You had to be present to win. When the cashier was satisfied that he had a winner, the payoff was made. The winner had to buy a beer for all the losers. This all proved to be a big get-acquainted event for electricians and later for all craftsmen.

As for Bill and me, Friday night was our night out. After an hour or so with the crews at the Illinois Tavern, we would go back to our house on Stanyon Street, change clothes, and head downtown to cash our checks at the Market Street Bank of America, which stayed open late. Then to our favorite restaurant, Original Joe's on Taylor Street just north of Market. It was the very best place for Italian food and steaks, and by far the most interesting restaurant we found.

We always sat at the counter, although there were tables and booths. Several cooks did the cooking just behind the counter. The cooks, all in white clothing and chefs' hats, would flip great pans of mixed vegetables, potatoes, etc., high in the air, never missing. Servings were generous and fairly priced. Patrons at the counter were a mixed lot. We might see people in tuxedos or evening gowns, fishermen, cabbies—just about all walks of life. It was quite all right to strike up a conversation with whoever was sitting next to you.

After dinner at Original Joe's, we had a few beers here and there and took in a floor show or two, but we would always go to a night spot at Fisherman's Wharf on the Embarcadero. It was a nice clean place and featured a bar, a small stage, and amateur entertainment. People in the audience would get up on stage and do their act. There was an emcee and a piano player. Usually, if an act was fairly good, the audience or the bar tender would buy the performer a drink.

Our act, "Two Bills from Boston," was a duet. We would start with some college songs, where we had loads of audience singalong. We would end with the "Whiffenpoof Song." It was fun, and we always had complimentary drinks in front of us.

At the shipyard we were making good progress on the two destroyers. They were launched as the USS *Maury* and the USS *McCall*, among the first to be built in the McCall class.

In recognition of our working well ahead of schedule, Bill and I, along with Pete Debes and a few other department heads, were invited to a party at the home of Harold Cheney, a member of the top management. Mr. Cheney lived on the Peninsula with his mother in a beautiful big house. Mrs. Cheney prepared many tasty snacks for us, along with cocktails. A friendly poker game topped off the evening.

Afterwards, we all milled around visiting. Pete Debes came by and pulled Bill and me aside.

"Say, I just heard that we have been awarded a contract to build two navy cruisers, and that you two and Harry Stone are to be transferred back to Fore River shipyard to help finish work on the aircraft carrier *Wasp*. After that, you will be transferred back here in time for completion work and builders' trials for the first destroyer," Pete explained.

The car that Harry and Bill owned was in good running condition, and we started making plans for the trip back east via the Grand Canyon. We approached Harry on our travel plans.

"No way," he said.

"How come?" Bill asked.

"Waal," said Harry in his Maine accent, "I've decided to leave Bethlehem and go back to my old job at Bath Iron Works in Maine."

"So okay, we'll all ride together." I said.

"Waal now, I'll tell ya, it's like this. Lillian and I have had a thing going on for some time, and I want to take her back with me. I want to leave for the East as soon as we can get packed."

"Sure, Harry," Bill said. "We'll settle up on the car in the morning." This was a big shock to both Bill and me, but in kicking it around, we both felt sorry for Harry, and in a way, for Lillian. Harry had been a loyal friend. This was probably as good a way to part as any. The next day Harry and Bill settled up for the car. We wished Harry and Lillian luck, and they headed east. We never saw them again.

The months in San Francisco had been good for both of us. We were supervisors, gaining valuable experience in planning electrical construction, as well as in communication, worker discipline, inspection, and other skills. This experience helped prepare us for our career objectives.

In June I flew back to Boston. Bill was to follow a week later. We took a two-week leave to relax, visit our families and friends, and do some fishing. Bill's boat, tied up to a dock in the Saugus River, was somewhat weatherbeaten but afloat. We fixed her up with a coat of paint. Bill proudly painted a new name on the stern : "Alice Marie," his San Francisco girlfriend. We took out a few fishing parties, had lots of good visits with old friends, and reported to work at Fore River.

Homecoming greetings were cordial but brief at the shipyard. We were told that a major push was on to finish our work on the *Wasp*. Bill was to do what he could to expedite shop work, and I was to do the same on board ship. As it worked out, they had lots of good supervision on the job, so for me it was back to working with tools wherever help was needed on the ship.

Bill and I shopped around and bought a car, mostly for the trip back to San Francisco. We found a used Buick limousine, with built-in wine cabinets and all; it was in excellent shape, and we got it for a good price. We delighted in giving Bill's dad a ride to work after a lunch at home. We would drive up to the West Lynn Works, as close as we could to the big gate. There was always a crowd out front. Bill's dad would exit from the back seat, slam the door, and without looking right or left, would stride past the guards and into the plant. His entrance was presidential. We could imagine the talk around the plant (egged on by Bill's dad) about the two Bills making it big.

The trip back to San Francisco did not go as planned. Bill and two electricians received orders to return promptly. I had some work to finish on the *Wasp*, plus one more builders' trial. We agreed that Bill would drive the Buick back west with the two passengers, and I would follow by air.

The first destroyer was just finishing dock trials when I arrived in San Francisco. Builders' sea trials were scheduled a few days later. The USS *McCall* was a beautiful vessel. The single stack was tilted slightly astern, like a speedboat, and with all the aluminum in her hull, she weighed less than other destroyers.

We passed under the Golden Gate Bridge and out to sea at dawn. The tests went well. Fuel efficiency was higher than specified and top speed was improved. All day and into the night the vessel was put through her paces. Everything was okay, and everyone was happy. Coming in under the Golden Gate Bridge, we were suddenly flooded by searchlights on the shore—just checking us out. It was another indication that our defense forces were being prepared for possible action.

Great Britain and France had declared war on Germany on my birthday, September 3, 1939. Japan was making friendly noises toward Germany. When we arrived at work the next Monday morning, four old World War I destroyers were tied up at our outfitting dock. They had been mothballed in San Diego, and they were to be outfitted and turned over to the British. We were told at a staff meeting that the German magnetic mine was being deployed in shipping lanes by the large German submarine fleet. The mines were raising havoc with British shipping, and twenty-seven ships were lost in the first two weeks of the war. Another fifteen were sunk in a four-day period. The magnetic mine was a German secret weapon, and there was no way to defend against it, until the British could examine one of the mines. Finally, one of the deadly German magnetic mines washed up on a beach in England.

It was a mighty brave team of experts who were able to dismantle the mine on the beach and find out what made it work. The mine was equipped with a relay system that would cause it to explode when it detected a change in the surrounding magnetic field. All ships generated a substantial magnetic field which varied in intensity from one part of the ship to another. We were told that most of these magnetic mines were anchored in place below the ocean surface, and a few were allowed to float free.

To protect a ship from these mines, the magnetic field of the ship had to be reduced to a degree that would not detonate the mines. The British solved this problem by designing a system of electric coils to encircle a ship; adjusting the flow of direct current through the coils would reduce the magnetic field.

The old destroyers (called "cans" by the Navy) would need one coil to completely encircle the ship at the main deck level, in addition to several other coils installed at different parts of the vessel. This was designated a rush job. Our crews would work overtime.

The cables were to be made in our shipyard. They would be composed of single conductor insulated wires formed into a bundle about three and one-half inches in diameter, with a canvas jacket enclosing the cable. I would be involved laying out the location of the brackets on the ships that would support the cable.

Bill would get up to speed making the brackets. The complete installation of hundreds of feet of cable, a special generator, and switchboard was known as a "degaussing" system.

The cables were finished and painted gray, and the brackets were welded in place on the first can. The cable, over seven hundred feet long, had to be installed without damage, and the Navy came up with a workable solution to avoid damage. They bussed a large group of sailors into the shipyard and guided them up to the mold loft, where the cable was assembled. One by one the sailors, spaced about four feet apart, had the cable lifted to their shoulders. There was a guide at the head of the line. Then the parade started: down the mold loft stairs, winding through the shipyard like a giant serpent, with two hundred fifty or more legs, then up the gangway and around the destroyer at the main deck level. When they stopped, they placed the cable exactly in place in the hangers already installed.

Work on the cans did not delay our construction schedule for the new destroyers. Mac Mageehon and Ernie Bernhagen were doing a great job. Mac had taken over work that Harry had been supervising. My time was divided between drawings for the new cruisers and the destroyers. Bill was becoming more involved in ship repair activity, work that he was very much interested in, in addition to his shop work. In ship repair and new construction, we were all committed to tight work schedules.

In January 1941, Bill and I were invited to another house party at the home of our boss, Harold Cheney. The format was much the same as our previous party. Harold's mother had arranged an abundant spread, with a variety of food and refreshments. We recognized some department heads; Pete Debes was back east, but there were a few strangers, apparently friends of Mr. Cheney.

During the evening of visiting, one of the guests came over to me.

"Are you Bill Bright?" he asked. He was a well-dressed, middle-aged man who looked and acted like an executive.

"My name is Austin Flegel. I'm an attorney for the University of Portland in Oregon. We're building a shipyard and have tentative contracts to build naval ships, provided we can assemble a staff satisfactory to the Navy. We need someone qualified to head up electrical engineering and construction. Your name has been mentioned as a possibility."

"Well sir, Bethlehem has always treated me very well. I have the highest regard for Mr. Cheney and others in management. However, I've always been interested in improving my position, and would be glad to discuss any suggestions you may have involving increased responsibilities," I said.

I gave an outline of my present and past duties with Bethlehem. He gave me his business card and asked that I call him the next week.

We visited briefly about the electrical part of shipbuilding, and I commented on the fact that the scope of electrical work covered such a wide spectrum, from temporary lighting used during construction to the most sophisticated electric systems, that it required specialists in several fields. We strolled over to where Bill Wild was chatting, and I took him aside and introduced him to Mr. Flegel, then left them to get acquainted while I circulated.

The phone call on Tuesday to Mr. Flegel's office went well. The highlight was his offer of jobs for Bill and me, building naval ships. My job offer was to be assistant chief electrical engineer in charge of all shipboard electrical engineering and construction. The chief electrical engineer then on the job knew general construction but was not qualified for naval ship construction. The offer to Bill was to be in charge of the complete outfitting and operation of the electric shop. I told Mr. Flegel we would discuss his offer and call him the next day.

This career opportunity came completely out of the blue. Our promotion at Bethlehem had advanced us to upper supervisory positions. Now this, within five years after leaving General Electric.

My first stop was to tell Bill about Mr. Flegel's offer, which really got his attention. After a short discussion, we agreed to try to get our friends and key employees, Mac and Ernie, to join us for dinner and discussion. We needed Mac's serious deliberation and Ernie's point of view.

At the restaurant, we first had a few beers and reviewed the discussions with Mr. Flegel and the Willamette Iron and Steel Company, or WISCO, project.

"If Bill and I accept the WISCO offer, will you guys join us?" I asked.

We all agreed that at Bethlehem we had the best jobs of our lives and could look forward to steady work for several years. We also recognized the fact that WISCO was a brand new shipbuilding facility, although the parent company was well known as a manufacturer of logging equipment. There would be problems in building and training crews at all levels.

"Well, I like my job, but I can see that I've progressed about as far as I can with Bethlehem. My superiors are young and highly qualified. The WISCO job would be a promotion and a chance to round out my shipbuilding career," I said.

"I'm in the same boat about job advancement," Bill said. "There's talk that I might be shifted to supervisor of swing shift at the shop. Building my own shop and crew would be a real challenge, but it sounds good to me."

"I like working on destroyers," Mac said, "and I've got a trained crew. Most of them worked under Harry Stone, so no problems. However, my main interest is in holding a steady job— this is my career. I'm a small-town guy. I don't much like big city life, so yes, if you guys go, count on me."

"I can't let you three guys blunder into a project way over your heads. I'd better go along and try to keep you out of trouble," Ernie said.

I would call Mr. Flegel the next day and ask if we could include Ernie and Mac, and if we could drive up on the weekend to visit the shipyard. We would give him our answer during the visit.

The telephone call to Mr. Flegel the next day revealed that he was president of Willamette Iron and Steel Company. He and his vice president, William Kettlewell, would welcome us if we drove to Portland on the weekend. He was agreeable to including Mac and Ernie with Bill and me.

The next Friday evening, we headed north in Ernie's Oldsmobile. By sunrise on Saturday we were driving through the beautiful Willamette Valley, with the Cascade Mountains to the east and the Coast Range to the west. We passed through miles of fertile fields, with pheasants, wild ducks, and geese flying about, seeing snow-covered peaks and beautiful rivers. We appreciated the lush Oregon countryside after living in crowded cities for years.

Our first view of Portland as we approached, looking down from the hills, was as pretty a setting for a small city as could be imagined. The Willamette River flowed through the city, with snow-capped Mount St. Helens and Mount Hood as backdrops.

After having breakfast, we met with Mr. Flegel and Mr. Kettlewell, and the chief electrical engineer, Bob Stevenson. Stevenson assured me that I would have full control of the electrical part of the Navy ship program if I accepted Mr. Flegel's offer. A tour of their facilities followed. Some buildings were under construction, but the engineering and shop buildings were finished. All four of us decided to join WISCO and to report for work in three weeks.

Back at Bethlehem we gave notice of our decision to leave, and were assured we could keep our jobs if we changed our minds, or chose to come back in the future. We all gave much more thought to our job change decision in the days that followed.

My reasoning always came back to the fact that I had advanced as far as I could with Bethlehem. The WISCO offer of the top electrical position in engineering and construction of naval vessels, when I was only twenty-four, was too exciting and challenging to turn down, even though it would have been much easier to stay with Bethlehem.

We were able to make the rounds and thank all of the people who had been so great to work with—all but Mr. Cheney, who was involved in meetings in the east. We left him a note of our decision, and of our gratitude for all of his courtesies. Mr. Cheney, Pete Debes, and a few others seemed to take a personal interest in my career.

In the months before the job offer from Mr. Flegel to join WISCO, my long-term career plan had included a couple more years with Bethlehem, saving as much money as possible. Then I hoped to find a position in marketing, to round out my experience before starting my own company, manufacturing something electrical.

This top WISCO position in shipbuilding (in Naval shipbuilding, no less) would provide once-in-a-lifetime experience in management and engineering, so I could not turn it down. I would delay the marketing experience. This proved to be a sound decision.

5

Shipbuilding in Portland

WISCO was an old, established, and highly regarded manufacturer of equipment used in the logging industry. An older office building and a huge, barnlike shop building, along with railway and storage areas, made up the original plant. Their acreage downstream and north on the riverfront was rapidly being transformed into a shipyard. A long outfitting dock was backed up by shop buildings, and a large mold loft structure and a new two-story administration/engineering building were complete, facing the highway. Several ship ways were being built leading down to the river, with adjacent plate storage and subassembly areas.

A representative of the U.S. Navy Thirteenth Naval District, Captain Whitgrove, was based at the shipyard. His civilian assistants included Cal Davis, electrical, and Tony Shores, machinery. Every one of the thousands of electrical drawings to be prepared in our engineering department was to be delivered to the supervisor of shipbuilding, after my examination and signature, for Cal or Tony to approve and sign. Once a construction drawing was approved, we could invoice the Navy for labor and material charged to the drawing.

My new job was a major leap ahead toward my career goals. Having full charge of such a large project was sobering and challenging. I already had a good idea how the electrical part of a Navy ship went together, and now I had much to learn about the administrative end of the process.

The engineering department was assigned the entire second floor of the new building. Electrical was on one end, machinery and piping on the other, and hull, structural, and ventilation departments in the middle, along with a blueprint room and a walk-in vault. Executives, purchasing, security and personnel took up much of the first floor.

Bob Stevenson, the chief electrical engineer, had his operations for shipyard construction under way for months before our arrival. Some drawings and specifications from the Bureau of Ships were already on hand. Stevenson was an easy person to work with, pleasant and helpful to me in my search for electrical talent. He also invited me to his home for dinner with him and his wife.

About this time in 1941, the United States entered the war against Germany. Rationing programs followed. We were assigned priority numbers for contracts with suppliers to obtain scarce material for ship construction.

Soon after the U.S. entered the war, we had big internal problems in our department. Bob had his personal boat, a 25-foot long cruiser, tied up at a company dock. He was accused of using government-paid company maintenance men to work on his boat during working hours, and investigations followed.

I avoided becoming involved and wasn't aware of all the details, but I knew that Bob was a good man and a straight shooter. Quite likely his use of government-paid labor was not premeditated, but the results were apparent. Bob resigned from the company.

Mr. Flegel called me to his office. "Bill, I want you to take over as chief electrical engineer, with responsibility for all electrical activity in the company, reporting directly to me," he said.

The major company change for me was to move into Bob's office. The electrical yard facilities program was well under way, and I would handle it in biweekly contractor meetings, as well as liaison with Stan Dye, the major supplier.

A major career change followed. I was advised that my position in shipbuilding was considered important to the war effort, so I could not transfer to another company or accept a commission in the armed services. If I chose to leave my position, I could only enlist in the armed services or be drafted. My career goals must wait.

I scheduled a meeting with our personnel department and reviewed our need for six engineers with strong credentials, whom I could develop into engineering department group leaders. We were told that personnel had previously canvassed the area for engineers with shipbuilding experience, and all had long ago been recruited in Seattle or San Francisco. We were lucky to find some outstanding people. Each was interviewed and screened for security, then sent to my office to be interviewed. Before long, I had six good prospects.

After weeks of advertising for electricians with shipboard experience, we found only one—Johnnie Grimes, a top engine room electrician. We then made the decision to set up a school to train electricians to do only one limited job on a ship, such as hooking up lights and switches, or installing electric cable. We received the okay to use a room at Oceanic Terminals at the north end of the WISCO property, and in this classroom we trained many people. They were taught how to do things the right way, to Navy standards and to our standards. The program worked out well. We had plenty of trained help and supplied trainees to other yards in our area.

Our first two ships under construction were cruiser minelayers, CM-6 and CM-7. They were designed to be lightly armored and fast, to speed into an area, lay mines quickly and accurately, and get out before the enemy could react. All the deck below the main deck was open, like an automobile ferry. Mines on cars were to ride on tracks extending the length of the ship. Electrically driven mine bogeys would push the mines overboard out the stern in preselected patterns.

We were all concentrating on pushing the job along on schedule when the word came to us that the ships were no longer a priority. Our CM vessels would now be completed as personnel transports.

Following the Navy's design change announcement, WISCO was awarded contracts for a large number of 180-foot-long sub-chasers and minesweepers. We were to act as the lead yard, furnishing drawings to other yards to build similar vessels. In addition, we were to convert large freighter hulls into aircraft carriers.

The CVE aircraft carrier program—several for the U.S. Navy and several for the British Navy—proved to be very interesting. We were to provide for all the aircraft activity common to the large fleet carriers, such as the USS *Wasp,* but on a smaller scale.

One problem we could not resolve concerned the equipment for launching the aircraft and the arresting gear—the means of securing landing aircraft. I found that the Philadelphia Navy Yard had developed most of this equipment. I received permission from the Navy to visit this highly classified area and spent a few days with their top engineers, making it possible for us to complete our part of the job properly and on schedule.

The first carrier scheduled for completion, HMS *Tracker*, was to be turned over to the British Navy. When outfitting was well under way, the British crew arrived. The Captain was a fine example of a British naval officer. He talked and acted much like my English grandfather, who had served as a gunner's mate in the U.S. Navy. We became friends in the weeks that followed and spent several evenings together. Some of the other officers were friendly, but few of the crew were.

The crew's attitude was apparent during dock trials, when the boilers were fired up, steam turbines were run, and so on. The British sailors were invited to stand by and watch or to operate equipment, but no one was interested.

"After all," one of them said, "our crew knows more about operating a ship than you people will ever know."

We took the *Tracker* out for sea trials. Everything was fine, but again the British crew was aloof toward our men. So it was back to WISCO to load with fuel and supplies. We said goodbye to the skipper and engineering officers, and they sailed on their way to New York to load aircraft for British forces in the Mediterranean.

At that time WISCO had weekly catered luncheons for department heads, during which we would discuss any problems that had cropped up. Sometime after the *Tracker* left, Mr. Flegel opened the meeting by saying, "Stores department has loaded sea spare parts for all four of the British carriers on the *Tracker*. We must recover the extra ship sets, worth many millions of dollars, before the scheduled sailing of the next British carrier. Bright, I want you on the first flight east tomorrow morning to meet the *Tracker* at the Army Base Pier in New York City."

"Mr. Flegel, I'd like to point out the fact that the electrical spares are a small percentage of the machinery spares, which include pumps, turbine rotors, catapult spares, and so on. The big money is in machinery spares," was my response.

"And I don't want to see you back here without those three ship sets of spares," Mr. Flegel said.

The chance of our reclaiming the spares seemed somewhere between slim and zero, but I would give it a try. At least I was on a friendly basis with the captain. Perhaps that was why the boss insisted that I go.

The bumpy airplane ride took most of the day. The following morning, after a ferry ride, I arrived at the Army Pier. There was the *Tracker,* being loaded with airplanes and supplies. I received permission to go aboard to meet with the captain. A sailor escorted me to his cabin. The skipper had a story to tell, even before I found a chair.

The ship encountered no problems until off southern California, where they had submarine contacts. This caused quite a stir aboard. Off Baja California, the ship's boilers shut down. There was no steam to propel the ship, and no lights. The crew was ordered to start the emergency diesel generators, so the boilers could be restarted, but, unfamiliar with the diesels, they used up all the compressed air in storage trying to start them. Finally, another small engine generator was located, and one by one the emergency generators, forced draft blowers, pumps and boilers were restarted.

The captain realized the incident was caused by lack of crew training. Everyone had learned his lesson the hard way.

"What brings you to New York City?" the captain finally said with a smile.

"Well sir, there has been an error in assignment of sea spares. The *Tracker* has her authorized spares plus those for her three sister ships. The three sister ships cannot sail without sea spares. I have been ordered by my management to arrange for their removal if possible," I said.

The captain explained that he lacked the authority to release the spares. Once taken aboard and signed for, they became the property of the Royal Navy. But he would immediately "send a signal" to report the situation to his superior in Great Britain.

After we cleared up our problems, I invited the captain and first officer to join me for a night on the town. We had a great time and a late seafood dinner.

The next morning, the captain called me at my hotel. His superiors were unable to authorize the release, and time was getting short, because aircraft loading was nearly completed. I called Mr. Flegel and told him the news. He advised he would contact Washington and told me to stand by at the hotel. After I waited another day, a call from Portland told me that the captain had received permission to release the spares, and Mr. Flegel was on his way to join me. A call to the captain confirmed the deal. I agreed to send the captain our list of spares to be removed.

Next, I had to arrange with a stevedore company to remove the spares, stowed in the lowest level of the ship's hold. They would be on the job the next morning. When Mr. Flegel and I arrived at the ship after breakfast, boxes of spares were already being piled up on the dock. Before the day was over, we had checked over all of the spares, arranged for shipment back to Portland, and bid farewell to my captain friend. The next morning my happy boss took a train to Washington. I relaxed on a bumpy airline trip back to Portland.

Although we no longer felt it necessary to attend night classes, Bill and I continued our close teamwork in our day-to-day

Although we no longer felt it necessary to attend night classes, Bill and I continued our close teamwork in our day-to-day operations at the shipyard. In Bethlehem's San Francisco shipyard, we had been identified as the "Two Bills from Boston" because many of our coworkers thought we talked funny, with our New England accent. The nickname followed us to WISCO.

If we were not otherwise involved, Bill, Mac, Ernie, and I always had lunch together in Bill's office, where we could discuss all aspects of the job in private. My job in engineering and administrative duties took up much of my time, often seven days a week. It was great to have this daily team input on problems and progress aboard ship and in the shop.

We were fortunate to have an outstanding group of employees in our various engineering departments. There were no interdepartmental squabbles. We enjoyed complete cooperation and became involved in bowling leagues, Christmas parties, and various good causes.

I was getting some valuable administrative experience at WISCO that I considered a plus in my preparation for someday building my own business. One important activity in which I became involved was purchasing major electrical equipment for the ships we were building. We had a purchasing department headed by Charles Brainerd, who had several assistants specialized in various areas. We in engineering would originate the purchase requisition along with applicable specifications and send them to purchasing. They would then contact vendors for price and delivery quotations. The quotes would then clear back through us at engineering and the Navy before purchasing placed the contracts.

Many millions of dollars' worth of equipment were regularly purchased, so we in engineering, who prepared the purchase specs, were the target for all the salesmen. Purchasing tried to screen salesmen before calling me for an appointment. I had many opportunities to judge who was a good salesman and why, and who was terrible and why. This experience gave me lots of know-how and confidence in my later career.

When certain naval vessels on duty at sea required major shipboard repairs, they were ordered into a particular shipyard for the repairs, plus as many design improvements as the Navy's allotted port time would allow. In order to determine the number of repairs that could be accomplished within a period of time and the cost, we had arrival conferences, originally at the dock in our own shipyard. The conference aboard ship would last all day, and involved the heads of WISCO electrical, hull, and machinery departments. It was a treat to deal with the crews in port after their long months of sea duty. We always tried to sneak in some extras, such as bunk lights or radio speakers, to make life somewhat easier for the crew.

Then someone had the cornball idea that the Navy could save one day of port time if we department heads were driven to Astoria, at the mouth of the Columbia River, the day before the scheduled arrival of the vessel. We could ride out on the pilot boat with the bar pilot, board the vessel, and have our arrival conference on the way up the river, usually overnight. The little pilot boat would bounce its way over the several miles of the Columbia River bar to the waiting vessel somewhere beyond the pilot ship. We then had the athletic challenge of boarding the Navy vessel by jumping onto a Jacob's ladder attached to the larger vessel, as it bounced up on a swell at the same time the smaller vessel bounced down.

We often spent all night inspecting, sketching, listing, and discussing. Usually the captain was so happy to have us aboard, he would break out some cheer to celebrate, which we appreciated.

Bill had arranged a deer-hunting trip over a long weekend, inviting me and two other men from the shipyard. I was probably included because I preferred to goof off in camp and do the cooking while the other guys tore off through the woods, sometimes scaring animals my way, so I could shoot them without leaving camp.

Our camping agreement was that I would do the cooking. The others would take turns doing dishes, camp cleanup, and other chores. But anyone who complained about the cooking would have dish and clean-up duty that day.

Bill and I had a chance to reflect on our career progress around the fire at night. We had advanced a long way in a short time. We arrived at the conclusion that luck had something to do with our promotions, but that our career planning and our "eager beaver" team approach to our jobs had a lot to do with it too. Also important was our priority to become acquainted and friendly with our supervisors and our fellow workers. Bill's early acquaintance with Pete Debes at Bethlehem and my friendship with support crafts aboard ship allowed us to outperform some other electricians. The combination of our Fore River achievements resulted in our promotion to San Francisco.

At the end of day two in camp, Ernie dragged in last—dirty, sweaty, no luck. He opened a beer and took a big spoonful of yesterday's stew—scorched in an open pan waiting for cleaning. Ernie spit out the stew, yelling "This goddamn mess tastes like bear shit!" He finally looked at the three of us sitting around the fire grinning and said, "Sure was good though." Ernie did clean-up duty anyway.

Each of my group leaders had different sporting interests, and I tried to spend some time after work with each of them, as our schedules would allow. Hew Milhollin, our power systems group leader, liked to fish, particularly at Spirit Lake, a beautiful, remote lake in southern Washington at the foot of Mount St. Helens. On an agreed day I would drive by Hew's house to pick him up. He would always have two meat pies (his wife called them "pasties") just out of the oven, in a box to keep them warm, plus a six-pack of iced beer in a fish pail. At the lake we would rent a boat, and drift out on the crystalline blue water, put our lines out, drink cold beer, and munch on the delicious pasties. And sometimes catch a lake trout.

Ed Reichwein, our lighting systems group leader, loved to play golf during warm weather. In late fall and winter, it was steelhead fishing in Oregon's swift coastal rivers. One day after a round of golf, Ed told me he was going to change jobs. He was interested in the electric utility industry and was taking a job as engineer for a small electric cooperative in Vernonia, Oregon. We were all sorry to lose Ed. We gave him a party and a grand send-off. We would continue to get together for golf and fishing.

After a year or so, Ed called to say he had again changed jobs and was now working in Seattle as a sales engineer, dealing with electric utilities. He was visiting Portland with his boss.

"Why don't you have lunch with me and our president, Mr. Hartzell?" he asked.

I was free and joined them for lunch. Mr. Hartzell, who preferred to be called "Pop," was extremely interesting. His company, Maydwell and Hartzell, had offices in the principal West Coast cities. He represented major manufacturers producing products for the electric utility industry, including nearly all material and equipment necessary for building power lines. His territory extended roughly from Canada to Mexico, from the Rocky Mountains to the Pacific Ocean. He said he was always on the lookout for talent, and if I would ever consider being a sales engineer, I should come to see him first.

Hew and I continued to visit Spirit Lake over many years. On what proved to be our last fishing trip there, after our pasties and beer fishing trip we spent some time visiting with Harry Truman, the man who rented boats. He was a thin, grizzled old man who lived a hermit's life in a cabin on the lakeshore. He had a small dock out front of the lodge, with a few boats tied up, and he sold fishing gear and bait and rented his boats.

Harry was fairly busy on the weekends, but Hew and I would try to get there during the week, and we almost always had the lake to ourselves. Harry always had a story or two to tell us, and we would respond with our latest.

On this last visit, Harry invited us into the lodge for a drink. There was a line of liquor bottles on a shelf behind his little counter, and we sat and chatted. He had family nearby in southern Washington, but he preferred to live in the silence and beauty of the lake at the base of snow-capped Mount St. Helens. He had a little trouble with his speech, and he detested the "dudes" that came to the lake on weekends and acted high and mighty, looking down on him in his old clothes. He told about one dude who had experienced some trouble with the equipment Harry had rented him; the dude was so mad Harry thought he would have "appleploxy."

A few years later, Mount St. Helens started acting up. The intensity of the earthquakes increased, and there were eruptions of steam. Family and friends, state and federal officials, all pleaded with Harry to leave the lodge, but he refused. In May 1980, one cubic mile of the top of the mountain blew off. Harry, the cabin, and the landing were buried under hundreds of feet of dirt and debris.

Spirit Lake became clogged with ash and dead trees, no longer a place to spend a lazy afternoon fishing for lake trout. The loss to Hew and me, along with hundreds of other visitors to the area, was two jewels—Spirit Lake and Harry Truman.

After the allied invasion of Normandy in 1944, the war in Europe began winding down, at least in the naval and Merchant Marine areas. The Navy and the Bureau of Ships seemed to place increasing pressure on West Coast shipyards to move up schedules of construction and repair to build up the fleet for the expected invasion of Japan. At WISCO, there was an order that our department heads were required to take turns, on a rotating basis, as night yard superintendents. We were to stay in the yard all night one night every week, and to make the rounds through the yard every hour or so, to make sure our swing shift and graveyard shift employees were all working.

We would find people loafing in all sorts of hiding places—inside tanks in the pre-assembly area, hiding in big pipes or under tarps. We would check their employee badge numbers and let them sleep to rest up for their employment termination the next day. If there were outfitting problems that came up, we were expected to solve them, and to keep the jobs moving. The additional work began causing health problems for me.

I started having sick spells for the first time in my life, taking shots and penicillin pills. The doctor told me stress was the problem.

"Why don't you come down to my duck hunting cabin near Scappoose Friday night for a Saturday morning hunt?" Mr. Flegel said after I told him of my health problem.

"Great, thank you," I said, "but can I bring along Bill Wild and two of our engineers?"

"OK, see you there," he replied. The two engineers I had in mind were our hunting pals, Ed Sturba and Bob Huget. The guys jumped at the chance to hunt with our company president.

Actually, this hunting date was exciting for all of us. The closest town to his lodge was Scappoose, a farming area about fifteen miles northwest of Portland. Between Scappoose and the Columbia River were lowlands and Columbia River backwaters and sloughs, just the setting for duck and goose hunting. The lodge had been built on a river barge, which had been towed to the slough when the river was high and then grounded. It had a kitchen, a large dining/living area, two baths, and several bedrooms. A small lake was nearby, with duck blinds around it. The lake had been planted in duck wheat and other goodies that the ducks and geese liked to feed on. The area was well away from civilization. The land was flat and swampy, with clumps of cotton-wood and alder trees.

We arrived at dusk, too late to hunt, so we went aboard, made ourselves at home, and dined on beer and sandwiches we had picked up along the way. After a while, Mr. Flegel arrived and suggested a poker game. We played a friendly game and enjoyed some of Mr. Flegel's beer supply. There was no big winner, but Mr. Flegel lost money. I reminded the guys that beating the boss at poker was no way to advance in the company.

Before sun-up we were in the blinds. With daylight came a dense ground fog, cutting visibility to about six feet. We could hear the wind whistling past the ducks' wings as they sailed into the lake, passing just over our heads, but we could not see to shoot. One by one we gave up and went back to the lodge.

Mr. Flegel was still in bed. We scrounged around the kitchen and found bacon, eggs, bread, and coffee, so we proceeded to cook and enjoy our breakfast.

When we were nearly finished, the boss made his appearance, not looking his presidential self in pajamas. He was unshaven and had mussed hair.

"Of all the rotten guys I've ever met, you four take the cake," he said. "You came to my lodge, shoot my game, eat my food, drink my beer, and take my money at poker."

"If we make you some bacon and eggs and pan-fried potatoes with toast and coffee, might you change your opinion of us?" I asked.

"Not a damn thing less!" he said.

Before leaving, he asked me if I would like to join him at lunch with Damon Trout the next week. Damon was a local businessman who operated a large electric motor repair facility and did some ship repair. He had an elaborate suite on the second floor of his shop, complete with a well-stocked kitchen and a Philippine cook/waiter. An invitation to lunch at Damon's was not to be taken lightly. On my two luncheons there previously with Mr. Flegel, the conversation had been mainly political, but they both quizzed me about Bureau of Ships and maritime practices, and battle damage I had inspected on ships at Navy yards.

On this particular day our host and Mr. Flegel were excited about a plan to establish a factory in Shanghai, China, to build fractional horsepower electric motors. Everything about the project looked favorable to them. The only problem was whom they could trust to send to China to set up the plant. None of Damon's employees was available. So both of them started leaning on me to get their motor show on the road. I would go to China, set up a plant, and train the work force. A nice salary and bonus were part of the deal.

"Thanks for the compliment, but I know absolutely nothing about manufacturing motors, or foreign access to China's markets. It would take months to prepare for such a project. Also, I have an important job at WISCO to complete, running the electrical department," I said.

It was then that Mr. Flegel pointed out the lack of contracts beyond the few ships we had left, and the fact that we would be looking at only ship repair in the future. We decided that I would make a four- or five-week study, and we would get together again early in the new year for further discussion.

It was time to do some serious thinking about my immediate future. I was twenty-eight years old and had completed eight years in shipbuilding, progressing from electrician to responsibility for everything electrical in the shipyard. There would always be a future in ship repair, but no real chance to continue in new construction beyond a few months. It probably was time to move along to something new that would benefit my ultimate career goal—my own business.

Decision time. Once again it was necessary to decide whether or not to leave an excellent position with friendly co-workers, in an industry I was completely familiar with, to prepare a work plan for the next time period before starting a business. I had made the right decision to leave General Electric and Bethlehem Steel. I was confident it was time to leave WISCO.

My choices were quite limited. Our country was still at war. My job at WISCO was considered critical to the war effort. I was frozen there, legally prevented from changing shipyards or accepting military commissions. If I quit my job, I could be drafted. I understood it would be possible to enlist in the Army as a private for eighteen months, which would certainly be a change of lifestyle. However, it would give me an opportunity to give some thought to a plan for the next few years before starting a business.

A visit to the Armory in Portland confirmed the eighteen-month enlistment. I signed up and was given three months to get my affairs in order.

"What branch of the service would you prefer to serve in?" asked the recruiting officer.

"I would prefer the engineers, sir," I replied.

"They'll probably put you in the infantry—we're short of infantry enlistments."

I met with Mr. Flegel, and we again discussed the Shanghai project. "Sorry, I don't feel qualified to handle it in a timely fashion. Perhaps you should recruit someone from the motor industry, " I said. "I've decided to put my department in order, and turn in my resignation in the near future." I reminded him that Bill

Wild was highly qualified to run a ship repair facility. I also expressed my deep appreciation for the many courtesies he extended to me through the years at WISCO.

Mr. Flegel ran for governor in Oregon in 1948 but lost to Douglas McKay. Later he was appointed ambassador to India. Not only did he experience a very satisfying tour of duty; in addition, the Indian government, in recognition of his service, presented him with a young elephant, which he gave to the Portland Zoo.

My resignation from WISCO took effect April 1, 1946. The Army had given me until June 29 to report. My Plymouth headed east for a leisurely trip, visiting family and friends all the way to Boston, then back west to San Francisco to visit friends, and then north to Portland.

6

My Introduction to the Electric
Utility Industry

The eighteen-month enlistment in the Army went by very quickly. After I and about a thousand other infantry troops disembarked from the troop transport in Japan, we set up a tent city on the hillside near a former Japanese Army base at Zama.

On the second day I was promoted from private to staff sergeant and assigned to the Adjutant General Department. My orders were to report to the 8th Army Automotive Maintenance School at Fuchinobe, located in a major Japanese Army base that the United States had taken over. I was placed in charge of all utilities and was to report to the base commander, Colonel Tom McGregor.

The duty was challenging in that I operated my own department, reporting only to the colonel. I met many fine career Army men, as well as other short-term enlistees like myself, who appreciated an interlude in a busy life to rethink career goals.

Army life was interesting. The days were always busy, but the weekends were usually free. I had plenty of time to think about the future and ponder the questions of how, when, and where to start my company, as well as exactly what to manufacture for the electric industry. What about financial, legal, and accounting? But the major question was sales and marketing. Should I try for a job in sales to electric utilities to learn all about the industry marketing and sales?

B ack home again in Portland, after an honorable discharge from the Army, I set up a heat pump business for some old friends. Then I called my ex-employee, the engineering department lighting group leader, Ed Reichwein. Ed was still enjoying his sales job in Seattle and was interested in hearing about my Army life. We decided to meet for dinner in downtown Portland on Friday.

After hearing all the details of infantry training, voyages on troop ships, and Army life overseas, he asked me about my future plans. I told him my Army service involved quite a lot of electric power distribution experience. "I sat on the U.S. Army Corps of Engineers Power Allocation Board in Tokyo," I said. "Also, the base I was assigned to depended on Army field generators for power because of the inadequately installed Japanese underground power system, and it was necessary for me to build a new overhead power distribution system, replace and add transformers, and manufacture my own power fuses. I would like to learn more about the electric utility industry. You've had a couple of years experience as a sales engineer in the industry. Should I consider sales engineering for a career?"

Ed explained he enjoyed a great sense of freedom in his job. He covered part of Washington state. He appreciated the high caliber of his customers in the electric utilities, the daily challenge to secure his share of the business in a competitive market, and yes, he was doing quite well, with a good salary and bonus arrangement.

"You remember our lunch with Pop Hartzell? Why don't you see if he has any openings? Remember, he asked you to check with him first if you ever were in the market for a sales engineering job," Ed said.

My telephone call to Pop Hartzell the next day resulted in an appointment to meet with him in his San Francisco office the following Friday morning. There were lots of questions in my mind about the electric utility industry, and about the function of a company like Maydwell & Hartzell within the industry.

My career goal continued to be the establishment of my own company. Perhaps experience as a sales engineer would help me identify products I could someday manufacture for the industry. At the very least, I'd learn something about sales and marketing. Perhaps I would also have opportunities to visit factories and study their organization. What made a factory successful? What caused another to fail?

At 9:00 A.M. on Friday, I was in Pop's office in a two-story warehouse/office building in downtown San Francisco. We visited until 11:30, then went to Pop's exclusive men's club for lunch, and back to the office again for more talk.

The starting salary was low, but fair enough considering the fact that I would be starting from scratch as a sales engineer. If salary was my major interest, I could have hired on again at Bethlehem's Union Iron Works building ships there in San Francisco. My salary at Maydwell & Hartzell would increase after six months—about the average time to break into this line of work. Pop said I would start in the Seattle office. Ed Reichwein was in line to advance to Seattle district manager.

"What are the prospects for advancement?" I said.

"The next opening for district manager will probably be in Portland. If you do well in Seattle, I'll want you to take over the Portland district," Pop said.

He went on to say that at that time all corporate shares had been issued. His personal stock holdings were barely enough to maintain control. Because of the company's record of strong earnings in the past few years, stockholders were reluctant to sell any of their shares. If shares became available, he would let me know.

We had no written employment contract—just a handshake. Pop seemed to be a man of his word. I agreed to start in Seattle as a sales engineer on January 2, 1949. I was thirty-one years old, excited about the prospects, and eager to get started. Pop escorted me out into the general office and introduced me all around. His vice president of sales was a man named Fred Mulvany, a pompous, dapper, thumbs-in-vest individual with wavy gray hair, glasses, and a haughty demeanor.

The office manager, a vice president, was the opposite in personality. Eugene Braun was relaxed, congenial, and competent. Fred and I never did get along, but I became good friends with Gene, and with Pop, who later invited me to spend the weekend at his lovely home on the Peninsula, not far from the Stanford campus.

The job became more and more interesting as I gained insight into the electric utility industry—an industry that many of us took for granted. As a source of energy useful to man, electricity had been around for a relatively short time, just since the late nineteenth century. Many of the older generation then had spent their youth, as I did, with kerosene lamps.

The business of generating and distributing electric power was one of the most capital-intensive of all industries. In order to service their huge debt, electric utilities usually operated in exclusive franchised territories awarded by city or county governments, for periods of fifty years or more. The utility normally returned a percentage of its customer billing dollars to the towns and cities in which it operated, as a franchise fee. There were several categories of electric utility companies, owing to differences in service areas, and different methods used to finance their debt.

After I returned to Portland from the visit with Pop Hartzell, I stopped at WISCO to visit Bill Wild. Things had changed in the two years since I left for Army duty. Bill was extremely busy in the ship repair operations. He appeared somewhat drawn and uptight, not his usual relaxed and outgoing self. We discussed the business of bidding against other companies for ship repair contracts. He enjoyed the challenge of beating the competition and improving on his own time/dollar price bids after receiving a repair contract.

I told Bill I had decided to go into sales and marketing, representing electrical manufacturers in the electric utility industry. This experience should prepare me to start my own company as a manufacturer in a few years.

7

An Exciting Assignment as a Sales Engineer

The morning of January 2, 1949 began with my arrival at the office of Maydwell & Hartzell (M&H). The office was located in a multistory office/warehouse building in downtown Seattle, handy to the ferry terminals and principal highways. One large office on the fourth floor was sufficient space for the district manager, a male secretary, and two sales engineers, along with the usual office furniture. Ed Reichwein introduced me to district manager Dick Harris and to Jack, the secretary. The plan was to spend the first week in the office and to begin customer visits the following week.

Training for sales engineer was as varied, I would expect, as there are different types of businesses. My job training consisted of one week in the office with Ed, discussing high points of the electric utility industry. We also discussed the manufacturers that M&H represented, along with some of their product line highlights. It was obvious to me that much of my knowledge of the job would need to be developed by a study of catalog material, and by asking appropriate questions.

The second week started on Sunday with a drive east over the Cascade Mountains and on to Okanogan in north central

Washington. The weather was clear and cold, with lots of snow along the roadside, but bare and dry on the highways. We checked into a small hotel and relaxed after dinner, ready for an early start on Monday, when we were scheduled to meet with my first power company purchasing agent.

At the power company, Ed introduced me all around, telling the purchasing agent and engineers that we had worked together for several years in a large engineering department, and stressing some of what he considered my unusual capabilities. Ed repeated his introductions at other power companies during the day, all very helpful to me in adapting to a new career, learning the ropes from a trusted friend who was obviously well liked by his customers. We ended the first day driving through a snowstorm to our next overnight hotel in Spokane.

Ed and I shared the accounts in the state of Washington. I would take one week-long trip each month, then take day trips for two weeks, followed by a week in the office to catch up on paperwork. Ed's job was covering large accounts locally, so he could take over as district manager when Dick retired.

After the second week at M&H, Ed and I took a few one-day trips together, usually for some specific purpose, such as filing a very complicated bid where we needed time to discuss options. Beyond that, I was on my own. I gradually became acquainted with more and more customers. And gradually my understanding increased about application of the various products we represented for electric utility systems.

Soon it became obvious that a factory representative really has two masters. He owes allegiance to his employer, who pays his salary and expenses, but also to his customers. Customers must have complete confidence that the rep will protect their interests in negotiations with the factories. If the rep does his job right, the customers will purchase more from his factories, resulting in more income to his employer.

The territory assigned to me covered some of the most beautiful parts of the Pacific Northwest, extending from Seattle to Spokane, and from south central Washington to the Canadian border. Also included were the small utilities on some of the islands in Puget Sound.

On my new job I realized every day the importance of the experience I had gained in my position at WISCO. Although in a completely different field there, I had interviewed a large number of salesmen, wannabe sales engineers, and really professional sales engineers. I appreciated the salesperson who would not insult my intelligence by making ridiculous product claims, and who was prompt and succinct in his presentation.

From the beginning, I was not completely untrained and inept as a sales engineer. To the contrary, my knowledge of the business was quite extensive, and I was determined to prove myself effective as a manufacturer's representative. The experience to be gained on this job would contribute to my success when the time arrived to start my own manufacturing company.

The months passed very fast. I was enjoying my job as sales engineer, and it proved to have many advantages for me as a person who preferred to use his own resources to excel in his job. There was a great deal of freedom, with no day-to-day supervision. It was necessary to be a self-starter, to set attainable goals, and be willing to learn day by day—just what it takes to be a winner.

There were pitfalls, however. The job involved a constant round of entertaining customers, with liquor included more often than not. It was easy to see that some salesmen I met were already lost to alcohol abuse, and others to bad personal relationships. Both weaknesses contributed to the failure of a high percentage of otherwise promising sales careers.

The week in the office doing paperwork and placing telephone calls was a welcome change of pace. One day I was talking on the phone to a manufacturer we represented about a special switchboard a customer wanted. The factory engineer asked how we wanted a certain telephone circuit brought out of the switchboard and my answer was "a jack termination."

What I meant of course, was that an outlet should be provided on the front of the switchboard panel to accept a telephone jack plug. The engineer understood my request.

We worked in one large open office, and we had a secretary named Jack, who was working at his desk and overheard me say "jack termination." When I hung up the telephone, Jack jumped up all upset, waving his arms and yelling that he had done nothing wrong. It took Ed an hour to calm him down. After that day, Jack was very formal and cool to me, no doubt still convinced I wanted him fired.

Early on, a problem became apparent: how to keep track of the dozens of customer locations around the state and the hundreds of individuals I had to deal with. Each utility had a purchasing agent, a chief engineer, a stores department superintendent, a distribution department superintendent, and so forth. Any or all might have questions requiring action. My solution for keeping track of everyone was a notebook.

All utilities I listed alphabetically, including mailing address, telephone number, along with all my contacts in each company by title. Then I made a notation of each person contacted by date, subjects discussed, questions asked, and any follow-up required. This information was noted immediately after each visit and reviewed just before the following visit. The notebook procedure proved to be the most valuable selling tool I developed during my M&H Seattle activity.

The first six months at M&H passed very quickly. I was working hard and as smartly as possible. Business bookings were very good, and the job was fun. I enjoyed the people I contacted in the electric utilities.

When the office mail was delivered on a Tuesday morning, it included a directive from our San Francisco general office, advising all addressees that Portland district manager Dave Hatten (another of my ex-employees) had resigned, and that Bill Bright had been appointed the new Portland district manager, effective the following Monday.

The Portland district included all of the state of Oregon and all Washington counties bordering the Columbia River. Pop had already kept his word, and after only six months. Here was my chance to organize my own district. This was also an opportunity to learn a lot more about marketing, and the business of representing manufacturers as their agent.

After kicking around my new assignment with Ed Reichwein, and promising a summary report of all my Washington customers for his file, I placed a call to the M&H Portland office to tell the secretary I would check in the next Monday. I then called customers and factories to let them know I would soon be in the Portland office.

Compared to the hustle and bustle of downtown Seattle, the M&H Portland office seemed detached from the business world. Downtown Portland was a ten-minute drive away. The Portland office consisted of space for the secretary plus two salesmen, and a private office for the district manager. I moved into the office cold, with no carryover at all from the previous manager. We never did have any contact with him—not even a phone call. However, Mary Tregaskis, the secretary, was the greatest. She knew all of the major customers, and all of the suppliers, and was a fast, accurate typist.

The Maydwell of M&H had passed away years before I met Pop. From what Pop told me about him, my sense was that Pop and Mr. Maydwell enjoyed a "team" relationship, much like Bill and me. The corporation was formed in 1898, with headquarters in San Francisco and offices in Seattle, Portland, Los Angeles and Phoenix. Since then other district offices had been added.

The M&H general office in San Francisco handled all banking, general accounting, and legal functions for all district offices. Monthly budgets for district sales volume expected for each of the manufacturers represented, along with district operating expenses, were also budgeted by the general office.

The districts otherwise operated more or less independently, performing sales and service functions, originating all correspondence to factories and customers, as well as invoices, contracts, and bids. All contract, bids, invoices and purchase orders were routed through the general office, and all customer payments were forwarded there.

In taking over the district office, the first project on my "to do" list was to arrange with Mary to assemble all customer purchase orders and correspondence for the previous two years, including sales records and general office correspondence. After a review, it was obvious that the previous manager's overall perform- ance was much less than was expected. The Portland office was deep in the red. Some manufacturers and customers were unhappy.

The first unhappy customer to make contact with me was Bruce Shavere, manager of Coos-Curry Electric Cooperative, a rural power company financed by the Rural Electric Administration, or REA. Bruce had recently moved to Oregon from an electric cooperative in Montana. Coos-Curry had electrical distribution along about seventy-five miles of the Oregon coast north of the California border.

Bruce was angry because M&H had sold him a mobile radio system to cover his entire service area and it did not work. He said if we did not show him some action, his next call would be to Washington, D.C.

"Hey, Mr. Shavere, this is my first week on the job here, but I can see you have an emergency situation and I will be in your office before noon tomorrow to get into your problem," I said.

Bruce was a big, burly, slow-talking man who had been a lineman/manager for years at an electric cooperative in Montana. He knew all about electric power distribution, but very little about mobile radio. I called the factory in the East from Bruce's office, and arranged for a factory engineer to leave the next day and report to him.

The factory assured me their engineer would stay with Bruce as long as it took to get the system operating to his satisfaction. The engineer arrived as promised, ordered certain replacement equipment from the factory, which he installed and tested, and Bruce released him, happy with the system. Bruce and I became good friends, having a meeting every month or so, and I often stayed overnight with his family in Coquille.

In my job as district manager, starting from point zero, the problem was how to get a handle on the major customers with no one to show me around. I knew the principal power companies, but none of the management or employees. Our largest customer was Pacific Power & Light Company. It was necessary to become involved with them soon. I called the secretary to the president and told her M&H was a major supplier, and that I was the new manager and wanted a few minutes with the president, Paul McKee.

The visit with Mr. McKee lasted half an hour. He knew my boss, Pop Hartzell. We discussed the fact that before enlisting in the Army, I ran the electrical end of WISCO. It developed that he knew my old boss Austin Flegel, so we got along just fine. He was interested in my contacts in Washington state.

"And for your future benefit, Bright," he said, "I strongly suggest you become a member of the Northwest Electric Light & Power Association. I'll look forward to our next visit."

As busy as Mr. McKee was, he took the time to visit with me and make me feel at home. He was a very fine gentleman. I made it a point to call at his office every few months. I never asked Mr. McKee for any help in our business dealings with PP&L, but strangely enough, every time I visited the president, the supervisory personnel in the operating departments seemed to know about it. There was no sign of resentment. I never discussed our meeting with anyone, but they were conscious of the fact I knew top management. I certainly recommended this approach to others in our company, provided there was no mention of product or their employees with management, and no mention of management in discussion with employees.

Through all this activity, my objective had been to establish the M&H Portland office as a reputable supplier, and to do everything possible to increase our share of electric utility business. However, there never was any question in my mind that this business development activity was excellent training for the future development of my own business.

My approach to sales was to become acquainted with all levels of power company personnel —from presidents, managers, and department heads to linemen. This sales activity proved to be very beneficial to the manufacturers I represented, as well as background for future success of my own company.

After my initial round of visits to the electric utilities, I realized that the Portland district was quite limited in sales potential. We had several well-established competitors who were selling similar products to utilities. The competition was clean. The problem was one of demand. There was just not enough demand to allow satisfactory turnover of our warehouse stocks. M&H would need more cash flow to pay our Portland expenses and end up with an annual profit.

8

Building Cash Flow with New
Product Development

Bonneville Power Administration (BPA), covering the
Northwest with their power transmission lines, was by far our
largest local electric utility. As a government agency, they were
required to deal with all legitimate suppliers everywhere, on the
basis of the lowest bidder meeting their bid specifications. BPA
purchased huge quantities of steel transmission towers, electrical
conductors, and porcelain suspension insulators.

The only manufacturer we represented that was of interest to
BPA was Victor Insulators. Their plant was located in Victor, New
York. Victor had several competitors, some larger than they, and all
were extremely interested in carload sales to BPA. However, since
BPA was right in our own backyard, it seemed possible to obtain at
least a part of this business.

Bonneville's purchasing bid files were open for public inspection. When time allowed, I would take notes of bid specifications,
lead time, and prices bid on various types and sizes and quantities
of insulators during the past year or two. I would also quiz
purchasing personnel about new transmission line construction
planned for the months ahead. This information I passed along to
Victor for planning purposes.

Soon we were receiving large contract awards, followed by more and more contracts. The dollar commission rate was low, but the total commissions were very high. Victor could now compete because they were able to program potential BPA demand into future production.

Victor was low bidder for two years, or close to low. Both M&H and Victor management were very complimentary to our Portland office.

An insulator manufacturer in Japan, one of the largest in the world, was low bidder by quite a margin on a very large contract. The Japanese claimed they met or exceeded all BPA specifications and were able to prove it. The Japanese competition put an end to our BPA business, but I found other ways to get around the insulator competition by combining sales to small utilities.

There was a large difference in cost of freight between insulator shipments by carload and shipments of less than carload quantities. The smaller electric utilities seldom had enough demand for a full carload, so they were forced to pay a premium for insulators. However, by reviewing estimated annual demand of many of our smaller utilities, we could combine the small orders of several utilities into carload quantities for us to order into our warehouse at much less cost to M&H. We could then ship the insulators out of our warehouse stock at an attractive discount to our utilities—a win-win deal for all parties. We booked a lot of business, and Victor named us their best national outlet.

The sales manager at Victor was Ralph Butler, a middle-aged, energetic, athletic, and cheerful person. On a visit to our office, Ralph had a suggestion: "You people do a great job for us in sales, in spite of the fact you've never been in our plant. Why don't you spend a few days with us, meet our people, see our processes?"

"You bet, provided I can get the trip authorized by general office," I said. My memo to Pop Hartzell resulted in a phone call, telling me to go ahead with plans to spend two days at Victor.

Victor, New York, was a small old town. The insulator plant, established in 1893, claimed to be the oldest in the United States. It also appeared to be the only industry in Victor.

Ralph said that originally Victor imported all of their clay from England, but later had developed U.S. sources. He introduced me to the president, Howard Failmetzger, and to all levels of personnel, quality, control, packaging, and shipping crews.

A sort of by-product of their insulators—coffee mugs —were also being produced. I was particularly interested in how handles were attached to the coffee mugs. The unglazed bodies of mugs were carried on a belt down a bench in front of women seated there, each with a supply of handles. With deft moves they moistened the contact part of the handle in a watery liquid, and pressed it, perfectly aligned, against the side of the mug. One of the women commented, "It's a sticking process." Later the mugs were glazed and the handles became a structural part of the mug.

The visit to Victor was my first factory visit. The importance of a factory sales rep visiting a factory he represents, and learning all details of the products involved in development, manufacture, testing, and other phases cannot be overstated. The rep can do a much better sales job. He also may apply what he learns to his own future company plans.

In the two days at the factory, I asked many questions, made copious notes, and gathered samples of insulator parts in various stages of the manufacturing process. The evenings were filled with refreshments, interesting conversations, and delightful dinners with the Butlers and Failmetzgers.

Back in Oregon, I visited many of my customers. The main topic of conversation was insulators and my Victor visit. Engineers and managers knew very little about the wet process porcelain insulator business, and interest was surprisingly high. Time after time I reviewed each step of the process used in the production of each model of insulator, along with test procedures.

One of the customers visited on my insulator promotion was Central Lincoln People's Utility District at Newport on the Oregon coast. Of all the smaller electric utilities in the northwest, Central Lincoln was exceptional in the degree of excellence of their management personnel. Their staff included engineers with operating backgrounds in large eastern utilities. Every visit would include lively discussions or debates about solutions to various operating problems. My input to these discussions was to suggest methods other utilities had employed to resolve similar problems.

A people's utility district (PUD) is an electric power company usually serving one or two counties, controlled by a local board of directors and a general manager. Operating capital was furnished by the financial market through the sale of bonds.

On this particular day I discussed my Victor visit with their manager, Larry Bauer.

"What are they doing about an insulator for use in highly contaminated areas?" he asked. He pointed out the fact that Central Lincoln's power lines ran parallel to the ocean for many miles. The insulators were covered regularly with wind-blown salt and dust and salt fog, which formed a conductive (the opposite of insulating) coating on the surface of the insulators, allowing electrical leakage across the insulators to the cross-arms and poles, frequently causing pole-top fires. The contamination problem extended along the coast and up to a quarter of a mile inland.

I had a few contaminated insulators analyzed at a local lab, and they found the expected salt deposits, along with dirt and a high percentage of alumina in the fine beach sand.

The normal contamination cycle began with fog rolling in from the ocean in the morning, coating the insulator surfaces with moisture. Later in the day the wind would pick up, blowing fine sand and dust onto the wet insulator surface. Soon the combination of wind and sun evaporated the moisture, leaving a coating of contaminants on the insulator's exposed surface. This buildup continued almost daily. A heavy salt fog or drizzle in late summer would cause power to leak across the insulator from top to bottom, causing a flash. As contamination increased, the surges became larger, sometimes resulting in a fire and power outage.

A check of catalog libraries at a local power company produced a brochure prepared by a large insulator manufacturer, detailing their exhaustive research and tests on insulator contamination. I considered their test procedures and conclusions questionable, and kept looking.

Possibly we should consider an entirely different shape of insulator, I thought. If the insulator could be formed in the shape of an inverted bowl with sufficient electrical creepage distance on the protected inside surfaces of the bowl to maintain the desired voltage, then the outside surfaces could become contaminated without causing a leakage problem.

The bowl opening at the bottom would need to be as small as possible to protect the inner surfaces. A sort of skirt could be formed and attached to the lower edge of a conventional insulator by a "sticking" process such as I saw used at Victor. The sloping sides of the insulator should help deflect airborne contaminants, and the enclosed dead air space on the underside would resist incoming air currents. This was the so-called pin type of insulator that was secured to the power pole's wooden cross-arms by a special steel bolt called an insulator pin.

I made a sketch of the proposed design, asking that someone at Victor call me to let me know if it was a feasible design. A week later, Ralph called, saying the plant would work on a development if I would come back to discuss field conditions. I called Pop, and he approved the trip.

At the factory, skirts were made, glazing and firing followed, then there were tests covering applicable industry standard electrical/mechanical values. The production people were satisfied they could produce the insulators in volume. The handmade samples looked a bit rough, but they worked. I asked Ralph to ship me twelve samples for field tests. When they arrived in 1952, I kept one, sent one to our San Francisco general office, and personally delivered ten to Larry Bauer.

Larry was delighted with the design. He had three groups of three installed in severe contamination areas, and kept one on his desk, where it remained permanently. No one was allowed to handle his first-of-a-kind fog bowl insulator.

After a spring-to-fall test period, the insulators were removed and examined. They showed no contamination on the protected surfaces. Larry ordered several hundred more for the next test phase. Other utilities followed, and many thousands were installed along the Oregon coast (see Plate 3). The insulators continued to give good service. Even Bonneville Power Administration became involved in suspension type fog insulators. Other manufacturers came on the market with copies of the fog bowl design.

The success of the fog bowl insulator project development gave me added incentive to be aware of other possibilities for new product development. Now I knew that I was capable of developing a new salable product—and it was interesting and rewarding to me.

Early on in the development of the fog bowl insulator, I felt I should apply for a patent. If awarded a patent, I would be expected to sign over all rights to M&H and Victor, because both had financed my time in development of the design. However, M&H refused to allow me to apply because of a clause in their agreement with Victor. Therefore, I concluded that any future development idea that I might have, I would keep until I started my own company. But I had a reward in the pleasure of driving along the Oregon coast and seeing the power lines supported by good old fog bowls, doing their job year after year.

Shortly after the fog bowl insulator project, I was introduced to a most interesting function of electric utility operations—the power distribution substation business. My interest was sparked by the fact that substations contained many items of equipment produced by manufacturers represented by M&H, as well as by the fact that my district needed more dollar volume. Substations had long been considered the heart of an electric utility. Basically, a substation is a fenced-in area containing equipment that allows the electric utility to tap into high voltage power transmission lines and transform the current to low-voltage power for delivery to a service area.

In a routine visit with Bruce Shavere, he asked me to travel down the coast with him to a small rural settlement to look at a substation that was causing problems. Practically every storm blowing in from the Pacific would shut down the substation and all power to the community.

This small substation was located not far off the highway in an area of small farms, within sight of a dozen or so houses. A new cyclone fence surrounded the substation, but everything inside the fence was a lineman's nightmare. Wood poles supported warped wood cross-arms and sagging high-voltage conductor (bare) cable buses. The power transformer had sufficient capacity but was not properly protected electrically. The substation was a mighty dangerous place for a lineman to operate, or even to walk into.

"Say, what can we do to replace this thing? How much would it cost? What is the best time it would take to replace it?" Bruce asked. We kicked around some possible solutions.

"Let's leave it this way for now. I'll make a sketch of an arrangement drawing, along with a price and delivery time estimate, and get it to you as soon as possible," was my response.

Back in the office I had a book of design details used by Bonneville Power years before to design their smaller substations. We also had references to various industry standards. Without too much trouble, I prepared a dimensional drawing, detailing a plan and an elevation view of the proposed substation. To avoid a long outage, I recommended leaving the existing substation intact while building the new substation. My estimated service interruption to transfer from old to new sub was only one hour.

Our bill of material listed all products to be furnished, including many of the manufacturers we represented. Making detailed drawings of the galvanized steel substation structure was necessary, then it had to be fabricated and test assembled, complete with all fasteners.

With all details in hand, along with an itemized list of material and a lump sum price for the package, I was able to get back to Bruce in three weeks. It took Bruce two weeks to review the proposal with his staff, the government and others. A phone call from Bruce gave us our first substation job.

As a factory rep, one frequently encounters opportunities for product development. Furnishing packaged substations (everything but construction) appeared to be a niche ready to be developed.

"Okay, Bill, go ahead, put a rush on the steel. Come on down to help the contractor lay out the footings, and keep an eye on the job for me." Bruce said. On our first job, we could not afford any mistakes or delays.

Thanks to the support of Schmitt Steel's president, Sam Lee, and his efficient steel fabrication shop, the structure went together quickly and easily (see Plate 4). The station was completed ahead of schedule, and Bruce was happy with the results. After all bills were paid, my office ended up with a reasonable profit. In addition, we had a new product line to increase our cash flow. Our competition was big—General Electric Company, for one—but being smaller, we were much faster to react and often at a more competitive price.

The M&H sales manager, screaming from his perch in San Francisco, accused us of all sorts of terrible things, such as not following standard procedure in applying markup to each product item sold. However, we preferred the method used in standard project costing—adding all costs plus a net overall percentage markup. He said we should have nothing to do with substations in the future. My response was to proceed to make up a brochure describing our substation packaging program, and to present a copy personally to all our potential substation customers.

Substations became a very valuable part of our product line, in spite of the sales manager's continuing objections. "Whatever legitimate business you do is fine with me. Just don't lose money," Pop told me. We later furnished dozens of substations and never lost any money. As a matter of fact, we made quite a lot.

9

The Nation's First Cable TV System

Early in my second year as district manager, I advised our general office that I needed sales help. My friend in the general office, Gene Braun, suggested I interview Hugh Dewar, who had previously applied to him for a sales job. Hugh lived near Portland and came in for an interview. We got along very well. He was a few years older than I and had been a career salesman with Westinghouse Electric Supply Company. Hugh was a gentleman of the old school, and he knew the selling business from top to bottom.

Hugh had lots of old friends among the utilities, which he had covered as a salesman years before while an employee of WESCO. We were able to split up the territory, much as Ed and I had done in Seattle. Hugh was fun to travel with and knew how to do a good job for both his customer and M&H.

Hugh and I agreed in one of our discussions that a factory sales rep who has a career goal as an entrepreneur has the opportunity to check out small businesses that fail—and why. The vast majority do fail. These are valuable real-life experiences important for the future entrepreneur to remember.

On a Friday afternoon in the 1950s, Hugh came into the office from a several-day trip along the coast to catch up on some paperwork. He had a story to tell about an old customer friend he happened to meet in Astoria. Hugh had met Ed Parsons in the old days when Ed was maintenance engineer in a sawmill at Cascade Locks, Oregon.

Ed now owned a radio station in Astoria and was one of Oregon's pioneer pilots. He still flew his own plane and was considered a kind of electronic genius. He had built his own radio broadcast station from used surplus equipment he had gleaned from other radio stations' discards. He designed and built his own broadcast tower. His record library and radio ads and other specialty programs were doing fine for him. But now he was on to something new and exciting—community cable television. As his story continued, Hugh became more and more excited.

At that date, Oregon had no television stations at all. The closest TV station was KING-TV in Seattle. There was a freeze on the issuance of new TV licenses, while the government formulated a new basis of frequency allocation.

"Ed Parsons has figured out a way to receive KING-TV channel 6 Seattle, loud and clear, in Astoria," Hugh said. "This is a distance from the TV transmitter in Seattle of 110 miles, over the Willapa Hills and Black Hills."

"Did you actually see the TV picture he told you about?" I asked.

"No, but Ed has a TV set in his living room in a penthouse atop the John Jacob Astor Hotel in Astoria, and he said I could come up any time to check it out."

All this discussion seemed like pie-in-the-sky. We all had been told that the new TV signals traveled in a line-of-sight path. Sixty miles from the transmitter was possible for reception, but much farther away the signal traveled up into the stratosphere.

"Ed is right now delivering a strong TV signal to twenty or more homes in Astoria by looping cables from house to house," Hugh said. "All the people are delighted with the reception and have been enjoying TV for several months. He knows we're in the utility supply business and he needs help to expand his TV business out of Astoria. I told him he should talk to you." I told Hugh to make an appointment for us to see Ed the next day, if possible.

The following day we drove to Astoria and met Ed Parsons and his wife, Grace. Ed was a tall, lanky guy, fiftyish and fidgety. He turned on his TV set, and sure enough, it was good steady picture with clear audio.

"Look, Ed," I said, "you are showing a first-class picture. Is it a canned or tape-recorded signal or what?"

"No. You are watching a live signal. Here, use my phone and call KING-TV in Seattle if you want to confirm it."

"No, I believe you. But why not tell us how this thing got started and where you go from here," I replied.

Ed frequently had business in Seattle, and would fly up in his airplane from Astoria, listening to KING-TV audio during the trip. In 1948 he took along an instrument to measure the strength of the video signal from Seattle and on south. He discovered that the broadcast TV signal separated into vertical "fingers" as it traveled beyond the horizon, and found he could locate the strongest of these vertical fingers by flying at right angles to them.

While flying over Astoria, he noticed one strong finger over a familiar spot on Coxcomb Hill, which is about 595 feet above sea level and minutes from downtown Astoria. After landing, he drove up the hill and found a good, strong signal. As far as we knew, Ed was the first person to discover this complete finger principal; at least, he was the first to do something with it.

Ed built and installed a receiver at the spot on the hill, amplified the signal, and transmitted it by cable to downtown. He then built take-off converters to carry the signal to his customers' TV sets. This was the very first installation of community cable TV in the United States. This fact is confirmed by a bronze tablet presented to Ed, installed atop Coxcomb Hill in 1958, by Fred Ford, chairman of the U.S. Federal Communications Commission.

Before the evening was over, we made a deal. Hugh and I would help Ed all we could. We would negotiate so-called pole attachment contracts with electric and telephone utilities to allow Ed to run TV coaxial cable on their poles. We would work with our general office for a line of credit for Ed to purchase the necessary material to build systems in Astoria and the Pasco-Kennewick-Richland area in Washington.

We became involved because M&H Portland district needed additional cash flow. If we could get Ed's business growing, the sales potential for cable and supporting hardware was staggering. We represented companies that could supply the material. By spending some time to help Ed, we would in fact be doing our job indirectly as sales engineers—a win-win program for both Ed & M&H.

All went along quite well. We were able to negotiate pole attachment contracts with the utilities at a very low price, so Ed could run his cable anywhere. We also worked up standards for Ed to use in mounting cable, and for service entrance into houses. I spent a sickening morning over Roseburg, Oregon, with Ed in his plane while he squirreled around the sky looking for a TV signal.

As the system grew, Ed experienced more and more quality control problems in his manufacturing operation. Much more sophistication in design and test procedures was obviously necessary. We bugged Ed about this. He would need a source of capital to set up a proper manufacturing operation, but his capital was very limited. Hugh and I had some ideas on raising needed capital.

Ed's answer to most questions regarding technical detail was "no problem," and that was also his answer to our suggestions regarding manufacturing expansion. Ed did agree, after weeks of urging, to a meeting we had organized with some of his radio station owner friends and a well-known and respected Portland attorney whose practice included contacts with the Federal Communications Commission. Our objective was to discuss a proposal to organize a corporation, to raise at least $100,000 by sale of equity, with Ed retaining over 50 percent of the stock for his control.

The meeting came off as scheduled. All were in favor of moving ahead except Ed. No amount of persuasion could change his mind.

Not everyone is mentally suited to become an entrepreneur. Even if a person has vast knowledge of the product involved, along with the assistance and best wishes of friends and associates, without the necessary mental preparation for the project, the chances of success are slim.

"This is my company. I don't want anyone to own me," Ed said. We visualized millions of dollars flying out the window. Later developments in the industry proved we should have seen hundreds of millions going out the window!

During the winter, Ed's problems with equipment became so severe that his customers started to withhold service payments. Next, Ed could not pay his bills. We tried several times to contact him, but with no luck.

Then one morning I received a phone call from Ed's wife, Grace. She said Ed had a nervous breakdown, and she checked him into the hospital in Astoria. However, in the middle of the night, he sneaked out of the hospital, jumped into his airplane, and took off for Alaska. He had no plans to return. Poor Grace was beside herself, not knowing what to do. There was no money for payroll or overdue accounts payable.

My advice to Grace was to see her attorney and her accountant immediately, and I would be in to see her the next day. At that time Ed owed us seven thousand dollars, which was a lot of money then. My Portland attorney recommended an attorney in Astoria, Gordon Sloan, to represent M&H. We agreed to make every effort to get Ed to return to Astoria, and to call a meeting of the creditors to prepare for bankruptcy or receivership.

At the creditors' meeting I addressed, at some length, my reasons for recommending a receivership be formed, rather than bankruptcy. All creditors agreed. Judge Howard Zimmerman appointed me as receiver, with all assets to be turned over to me. So, if only temporarily, I owned the very first cable television system in the country.

I scheduled two days per week for Astoria. We were able to convince Ed's serviceman, Ken Classen, and his old engineer, Eino Rippa, who built the original equipment, to return to the shop and work for free until we could get organized.

We started removing and rebuilding the cable TV equipment, correcting major faults, and one by one we reconnected customers. I borrowed tools and test equipment from some of Ed's suppliers, who were hoping to be paid their overdue invoices some day. We even had a Mr. McGee from Newport ask if he could work in the shop for free, just to learn about Ed's equipment. He later received a franchise from the city of Newport to start his own cable TV system and became known as "TV McGee."

The fellows in the shop did a fantastic job of rebuilding equipment and restoring faith in the cable system. The main problem with Ed's original equipment was caused by changes in outdoor temperature and humidity, which we corrected. We did make up the employees' pay as the cash flow built up. Meanwhile Gordon Sloan was successful in convincing Ed Parsons to give Grace Parsons power of attorney. The business was a partnership, thus allowing Grace to transfer the property to me as receiver. Then, after weeks of trying in vain to get Ed to come back, we agreed to ask the judge for permission to advertise for bids for sale of the cable system.

Gordon and I both were awarded seven hundred and fifty dollars for our services, plus expenses. The creditors all received a percentage of their claims.

It was late in the day after a long court battle when the judge made his award decision. Gordon and I were both exhausted. Gordon suggested I stop by his house for some refreshments before leaving for the two-hour drive to Portland. Gordon, his wife and I relaxed and reviewed the extraordinary events of the past three months.

With all of Ed's great talent, he was obviously not prepared to be an entrepreneur. He could not trust others to participate in ownership with him. We three talked until the sun came up over the Coast Range.

Ed Parsons spent the rest of his life in Fairbanks, Alaska. He died May 23, 1989, at the age of eighty-six.

As for Gordon Sloan, then a partner in the law firm of Anderson, Sloan in Astoria, Oregon, he was one of the finest men with whom I have ever been associated. Gordon went on to become a justice in the Oregon State Supreme Court.

Hugh and I did all we could for Ed, and we were sad to see the failure of such a promising business career. As for M&H, we did sell many miles of special TV cable, and lots of pole line hardware, all of which helped build up our cash flow.

In my own future business, I would guard against repeating the mistakes Ed made in his manufacturing effort. The Ed Parsons program was a very valuable part of my preparation for an entre-preneurial future.

10

Becoming Involved as a District Manager

It was time to return to my basic job of representing manufacturers, rather than designing insulators or being involved in cable television. The largest manufacturer represented by M&H was the James R. Kearney Corporation of St. Louis, Missouri. This outstanding company was one of the true pioneers of the electric utility industry. It had established many product standards in connectors for electrical conductors, as well as high voltage fuses, fuse cutouts, and other items. Its products were marketed to electric utilities throughout the United States and in Canada, where Kearney operated a major factory.

My initial interest in Kearney was how they became so successful. The story I was told involved Mr. Kearney as a young factory sales rep calling on electric utilities back in the early 1900s. He noticed that when it became necessary for linemen, "belted on" high up on a power pole, to splice two copper conductors together, they had to have pots of molten solder hoisted up the power pole on a handline. This was slow and dangerous work, placing the linemen and ground personnel at risk of serious injury.

Mr. Kearney was convinced there was a better way to make a splice. He experimented with various clamps, finally concentrating on large bronze bolts. He cut a slot in the shank of the bolt from the end back to the head, wide enough to allow the bolt to fit over the copper line wire in a splice. He then turned a nut on the bolt threads to apply pressure to the splice, making

it possible to complete the splice quickly and safely without the use of molten solder. Old-timers in the industry called the connector a "Kearney." Others called it a "split bolt connector." It was a hit from the beginning. Many millions were sold worldwide, and they were being manufactured by competitors as well, eight decades later.

After developing the connector, Mr. Kearney showed rare business acumen and foresight by realizing that a strong marketing organization would be necessary for the success of a manufacturer in the fast-growing electrical industry. Also, he would need the best manufacturing facility to produce a quality product for sale at competitive prices. He accomplished both goals by searching out the best sales organizations in each marketing area of the country—people like Pop Hartzell in San Francisco.

He convinced each sales organization to invest money in the Kearney Company in return for exclusive sales rights to Kearney products in their sales area. The sales organizations would push Kearney products to protect their investments, while providing Kearney cash to build a modern factory without going into debt. Many product developments followed the split bolt connector and were pushed nationally by his sales organization, resulting in Kearney's maintaining a leadership position in the industry for decades.

Kearney held annual meetings of their sales representatives in St. Louis. My first attendance at an annual meeting was in the January after the Ed Parsons interlude. All the sales representatives were booked into the Park Plaza Hotel, which was connected to the Chase Hotel by a sky bridge.

Everything about the sales meeting was first class. The presentations, beginning at eight in the morning, were interesting and appropriate. Some talks were presented by Kearney staff people, and others by salesmen who had excelled in the selling of one product or another the preceding year. After 5:00 P.M. we were on our own. Back at the hotel, we all seemed to gather in two or three suites. Some would become involved in endless poker games. However, other groups would tend to relax, have a few beers, and talk shop. We all seemed to be interested in what was going on in our business world or in another person's territory.

As well planned and presented as the scheduled sales meetings were, many of us agreed the bull sessions with our peers from all over the country were of the greatest value to us in our day-to-day sales activity.

Sales meetings were frequently used to introduce new product developments. Kearney was the industry leader in new products for many years. One new product had an interesting introduction: the Kearney squeeze-on connector, developed to replace the split bolt connector, and to be installed with a hydraulic or mechanical tool.

However, the mechanical tool was not selling too well. Customers complained it was too clumsy. These reports reached Kearney's leading project engineer, Bill Olive, who prepared a film presentation of a lineman up on a ladder using the mechanical tool to connect incoming conductors to a building service entrance. The lineman on the ladder flipped the tool around like a juggler. He made it look so simple and easy to use. The film was shown to linemen all over the country. Once a lineman saw the film, he wanted to prove he was every bit as good as the fellow in the film.

The fellow in the film with the fancy moves was none other than my friend Petey Pederson, a Kearney hot line tool demonstrator. I traveled with Petey through the Northwest. He pulled a trailer behind his car filled with all kinds of hot line tools. Hot line tools were specially insulated to allow a properly trained lineman to work on electric power lines while the lines were hot, or energized.

After demonstrating and selling hot line tools for several years, Petey changed jobs. He joined an old mutual friend, Orville Dwyer, who had a sales agency representing Kearney. The agency became Dwyer-Pederson Agency, located in Lexington, Kentucky.

Before leaving the Kearney story, I must point out the fact that a factory sales rep did have the opportunity, while visiting factories he represented, to study their structure. Jim Kearney's perception of the need for a better way of connecting high voltage conductors resulted in the development of the split-bolt connector. His solution for raising start-up capital avoided bank loans and established a strong marketing team. These were lessons I learned and benefited from when the time came to start my own company and continue toward my career goal.

My involvement in Northwest Electric Light and Power Association (NELPA), was another learning experience. Anyone who became a sales engineer or factory sales representative soon was aware of trade associations and their importance in the business world.

On my first visit to the NELPA office, a young woman, Jeannie Faulkner, greeted me. She introduced me to the executive manager, Berkley Snow, an elderly gentleman, very pleasant and gracious. Berkley gave me a brief review of what NELPA was all about and invited me to become involved.

I seemed to be involved in NELPA from the very beginning, particularly in the meetings held in Portland. A hospitality hour was scheduled on the evening prior to the meetings. We suppliers were expected to pay for refreshments. It was the responsibility of the chairman of the hospitality committee to raise the money. In order to keep costs down, we provided only one bar, served by one slow but accurate bartender. This worked okay until we could get the system changed.

The hospitality hour was a winner from the beginning. It gave everyone an opportunity to get acquainted. Suppliers could visit with utility engineers, and utility personnel could visit with utility executives, and so on.

Shortly after I joined NELPA, Berkley Snow retired as its executive manager, and Alden F. Krieg was appointed new executive manager. Al was a personable young engineer employed by Portland General Electric Company. He was a talented leader and everyone's choice.

Under Al's leadership, NELPA soon became the forum for discussion of Northwest electric utility industry problems affecting continuity of service, safety of public and utility employees, standards for products and practices in overhead and underground power distribution. NELPA membership grew from several hundred to several thousand, and included employees of all Northwest investor-owned electric utilities, along with factory representatives and financial, investor, and other organizations dealing with utilities.

I considered NELPA my forum, a marketplace for making valuable contacts with all levels of personnel in all of the northwest investor owned electric utilities. Also, it allowed me the opportunity to know and work with my competitors, and to work together in NELPA to build something worthwhile.

As for my participation in NELPA, I was fortunate to be selected to serve on several committees through the years. Service on the NELPA board of directors was extremely interesting, followed by four years as vice president overseeing each of the four NELPA divisions for one year. I was president for a year and served a year as past president. My NELPA experience was a career highlight for me, as no doubt it was for all NELPA past presidents, many of whom were also presidents or vice presidents of electric utilities.

One of the advantages of a career as a factory sales rep was participation in associations such as NELPA, where you could become acquainted with leaders in the industry. Also in traveling around the state, other opportunities developed to meet important people.

For example, I made my monthly visit to Medford, Oregon, a trip of 250 miles, on a Sunday so that on Monday morning, I could visit the California-Oregon Power Company. One such Sunday evening I was sitting in the lobby of the Medford Hotel when I recognized U.S. Senator Wayne Morse relaxing, reading his newspaper. The senator was well known, as a vociferous participant in debate, earning him the nickname "Tiger of the Senate."

I interrupted his reading and introduced myself: "Here's a Republican admirer of a Democratic senator." We visited for some time, had dinner together, and arranged to meet the next day, when he would ride with me to his next appointment in Coos Bay on the Oregon coast, a few miles from my appointment with Bruce Shavere in Coquille.

Senator Morse had a world of exciting experiences and a knack for bringing them to life. I looked forward to the long drive to Coos Bay and more interesting conversation, but it was not to be. We no more than got under way driving west, when he excused himself and slept all the way to Coos Bay.

Several months later he rode with me on another three-hour trip to central Oregon.

"How are you able to shut everything off at will and just go to sleep?" I said.

"Well, it all comes with the job. I get totally involved in Washington and nap on the way to Oregon to be involved in a busy appointment schedule. Every word said in public is recorded, and frequent naps are necessary to keep my clock from running down."

It was particularly interesting to hear of Senator Morse's experiences as a member of the Small Business Committee, and his interest in encouraging growth of small business in Oregon. He was of great help to me in my future product developments. He repeated the invitation several times to visit him in Washington, or to call him if we had a particular political problem to discuss. Later in my business activity I found it extremely important to know personally someone in Congress, for guidance as well as muscle in dealing with federal problems or business prospects.

The Kearney experience was living proof of the importance of product development and marketing/financing expertise. The NELPA experience permitted me the opportunity to become acquainted with a wide range of industry leaders, all-important to a future entrepreneur. Communication and public speaking would also prove to be important: hardly a month would pass that I did not speak to a group about products.

It all began at lunch with my friend Virgil Solso, who was later to become president of Oregon Mutual Savings Bank. We enjoyed having lunch now and then at the Oregon Oyster House in Portland. We always ordered oyster stew made with delicious Yaquina Bay oysters. The best part was that Virgil loved the stew but could not eat the oysters, so I would have all his oysters and end up with double oyster stew. This day we talked about public speaking. We both were called upon occasionally to speak to groups. Neither of us had training in public speaking, but we felt comfortable speaking on subjects within our own industries.

How often I had attended presentations by well known engineers who obviously had no training in public speaking—unable to make a point or maintain audience interest! And we both had a gripe about certain other speakers we had observed, who used a speaking style involving arm-waving and hand signals to illustrate practically every sentence or thought. We wondered if we were doing something just as aggravating to our audiences.

"Perhaps we should look into some speech training," I said.

"I understand Toastmasters International is all about public speaking, and they have weekly sessions timed to allow working people to attend," Virgil replied.

After checking into Toastmasters, we decided to join a local club that met for breakfast at a downtown hotel every Monday morning at six. An objective of Toastmasters was to teach people how to stand before an audience and communicate a message in a manner acceptable to professionals in public speaking.

At first it seemed a crazy idea—to stumble out of bed in the wee hours every Monday morning and rush downtown to a hotel. But it proved to be an interesting and constructive experience. I remained with the club for several months until it interfered with my job. However, I enjoyed every minute at Toastmasters.

At the start, every member was provided with a course outline and instructions in public speaking. Our club had about twenty members. On arrival at the hotel meeting room, we took our place at the conference table and ordered breakfast. Then each member was handed a slip of paper with a different "table topic." The topic could be anything at all. Whether he knew anything about it or not, each member, in turn, had to stand and talk about his topic for two minutes.

Each week one person at the table was designated as time-keeper, and another person was designated to criticize the performance of each speaker. After table topics, some longer prepared speeches were scheduled. Criticism was always constructive. The person you criticized this week might be criticizing you next week. Proceeding on this note, everything at each meeting was constructive.

Our club included people from a wide variety of businesses, including one man who spoke poor English and worked as a janitor. The speeches went on without delay as our breakfast was served.

The speeches given by the members generally reflected their businesses and their life experiences, and were usually very interesting. We were coached on how to structure a speech, how to make an important point, how to maintain audience interest, how to stand, what to do and what not do with our hands. We became used to receiving constructive criticism after every speech, and to hearing the criticism of other speakers, and it took very little time to learn the fine points of public speaking.

By the end of the term, we had all the confidence in the world to stand before a group anywhere, any time, with little or no notice, and do a credible job of communicating with an audience. Even our fellow Toastmaster member who began the class speaking poor English and stumbling through a presentation was a far different person at the end of the term. He went on to form his own janitorial company and did very well. My banker friend, Virgil Solso, went on to become bank president. Others in our group made the news from time to time in promotions and advancements.

As for me, I really enjoyed the program. Talking in public was nothing new for me, but knowing exactly how to go about preparing and delivering a speech was all new and gratifying. The program certainly removed the nervous apprehension many of us experienced prior to the start of our speeches.

There was constant criticism about my real or imagined New England accent. I always thought we New Englanders pronounced our words the correct way. In my final speech I dealt with the business of pronunciation and enunciation of words in our language, and the variations in accents from one area to another in the U.S. The point of the speech was the fact that the Pilgrims landed at Plymouth Rock, a few miles from my birthplace in Massachusetts. Also, the Massachusetts Bay Colony was established at Boston early in the seventeenth century. This all took place long before the West was settled. Yes indeed, it was the people who migrated west who should resolve to make every effort to correct their pronunciation. I received compliments on my speech, but was politely reminded to work on my pronunciation.

11

The Challenge: Increase Sales Volume, Decrease Fixed Overhead

As mentioned earlier, we were constantly on the lookout for new business to help finance our M&H operations and hopefully, have a few dollars of profit for year-end sales bonuses. One approach to more sales volume was to keep reminding the large utilities that we were interested in supplying specialties that the large manufacturers considered unprofitable, such as odd sizes of pole line hardware. As a result, we began booking orders in good volume for cross-arm braces, steel plates, and bolts. Our friends at Schmitt Steel regularly made quality products and knew all about electric utility standards.

During a discussion of specialties on one electric utility visit, an engineer asked if I could suggest a source of aluminum pole gains. I said, "Sure: me."

When a lineman attaches a wooden cross-arm to a power pole he uses a sort of washer plate, called a "gain," between the cross-arm and the pole. The metal plate is curved on one side to fit the round surface of the pole, and flat on the opposite side for the cross-arm to rest against it.

A bolt goes through the cross-arm, the gain, and the power pole to hold the complete assembly secure. Normally, power poles were furnished with flat surfaces cut into the pole at standard cross-arm locations.

Our largest aluminum/magnesium foundry was Pacific Light Metals Foundry. Bob Miller was the president. I arranged a visit with Bob to discuss the possibility of his furnishing a cross-arm gain made from a high grade of aluminum alloy. He promised a quotation in two days, then took me on a tour of his plant.

We heard lots about aluminum and its many alloys, but very little about magnesium. Properly alloyed and heat treated, it was often substituted for steel in products where minimum weight was important, such as aircraft parts. The magnesium casting, equivalent in size, shape, and strength of a steel casting, might weigh as much as one-third to one-half less than the steel part.

The aluminum cross-arm gains were a hit, and utilities began ordering them by the thousands. For several years we had a lock on the market, until a competitor developed a gain made of plastic which cost less than aluminum and performed satisfactorily. However, Bob Miller and I had become good friends, and we had many long talks about my plans for the future.

Bob had devoted his career to metallurgy and, starting with very little, had built a nationally recognized company. He urged me to wait no longer—start my own company now. The Portland area was outstanding in the number and diversity of independent manufacturers, and I should have no problem in developing products to sell to electric utilities.

"Yes, Bob," I said, "I've had the urge to start my own company for years now, but I am determined to wait until I'm sure I have all the bases covered. I do have a career plan I'm working on, a plan that will hopefully allow me to avoid the mistakes many others have made in starting a company without all the essentials required, only to go broke in a few years."

In my second year as a sales engineer, I developed an entrepreneur plan that would prepare me to start my own company by my fortieth birthday. The plan was detailed in my business notebook, and frequently reviewed during the years that followed.

Much of my planning was influenced by failures of new businesses I had observed, and the reasons for their failures. I hoped that if I could establish sound prerequisites for starting my business, I could avoid some of these observed causes of failure by otherwise competent people.

First came the question of capital: how much money would be required? I would borrow no money for operating capital, but would have sufficient personal savings to finance operations for one year. If the company were not self-sufficient in one year, I would close it down and find a job.

At least two years prior to the start of business, I would become personally acquainted with an attorney, an accountant, and a banker, and let them know my plans well before I needed their advice. Access to these three disciplines I considered a necessary foundation for the success of a new business.

I would start my company as a manufacturer's rep, with a few good factories to represent and no employees. I would sell to electric utilities, but would not compete for manufacturers with my past employer. This sales activity should generate cash flow to finance company operations. As cash flow and time allowed, I would start manufacturing my own product line, while devoting all necessary time to the promotion of the other manufacturers' lines we would be representing.

I would continue to search for ideas for product development and patent possibilities, and continue my activity in electric utility associations.

This entrepreneur plan would be developed over several years and would take patience and determination, and I needed to keep my future goals in focus while giving M&H my best efforts to build their company.

The business of increasing sales volume was slow, and at times discouraging. The monthly profit and loss statement received from the general office indicated an increasing trend in sales volume, but a corresponding increase in expenses. The office rent was stable from year to year, but the public warehouse handling charges increased as sales increased. The in-and-out cost of handling products was eating up our sales profits. I considered leasing our own building and hiring our own warehouseman. This option, if financially feasible, might also cut down on shipping mistakes, an ongoing problem.

It turned out that there were quite a few office/warehouse buildings for lease in the area, but none that was just right for our needs. There was a vacant corner lot not too far from our office, at the intersection of two busy through streets. A sign on the lot said the owner would build to suit. Out of curiosity I called the number. It was Cal Bag Company, a local dealer in used metals.

The president, Maury Rosenfeld, invited me to stop by and discuss our building needs. I made a rough sketch of an office/warehouse layout and went over to see him. He was a very busy but pleasant person—an admitted workaholic.

The vacant corner lot in question was in trust for his two sisters. He offered to finance the construction of whatever we wanted in a building. His architect would develop the drawings, and he would make us a deal, based on his twenty-year mortgage of the construction cost on a net-net basis. We would pay for any increase in taxes, insurance, and inside maintenance. He would pay for any exterior building maintenance. His estimate of cost was well below our costs at Oregon Transfer Building.

It took very little time to convince the general office that we should go along with this deal, subject to their final approval of finished drawings and the lease agreement. The final drawings and lease were available in ten days. The cost was even lower than Maury's estimate, and we were under way. As it worked out, there were many more benefits to be realized in the future by operating from our own building than my original goal of reduction in overhead.

While the building business was going on, my secretary Mary told me it was time for her to leave the company and begin a family. Operating the office without Mary would be difficult. To find a replacement, I contacted the personnel departments of the local electric utilities for suggestions of someone available who could speak the electric utility language.

The following day a woman at Bonneville Power called with a prospect to interview. Her name was Laurel Pithoud, daughter of

Pete Pithoud, a well-known and respected power line contractor. Laurel had graduated from Oregon State University a year or so earlier and had taken a job at Bonneville, but was not comfortable doing routine clerical work. She wanted the challenge of a single-person office. She impressed me as being sharp, had adequate typing and bookkeeping experience, and, having grown up in the business of electrical contracting, she knew the language. There was time for Mary to familiarize Laurel with our forms and procedures. In no time at all, she was doing everything Mary had been doing. She really liked her job and we thought the world of her.

About a year after it was started, the new building was ready. General office had transferred George McMurdo from the San Francisco warehouse to our new warehouse. This helped us get started on the right foot. Now the Portland district consisted of Hugh, Laurel, George, and myself. The company name in large letters was painted across the front of the building. The busy traffic location gave our company a big boost locally—a sign of success, prosperity, and permanence. Even more important to me, our storage and warehouse costs were now fixed and much lower. We had the latest in office facilities, and George kept the warehouse in perfect order, thus ending our inaccurate shipment problem.

When presenting a new office to the trade, it was customary to invite customers to an open house. Pop Hartzell agreed to attend and to meet some of the electric utility executives. The open house was mobbed. Judging by the volume of cocktails, beer, and finger food that disappeared, it was a smashing success.

Throughout the negotiation and construction phase of the new building, we did not have a single moment of disagreement or problem with Maury, or with any of his people. He was a man of his word. It was not long after completion of the building that Maury passed away. M&H operated out of the building for the entire twenty-year lease period.

As noted above, the new building gave our district office an appearance of success and permanence. This quite likely was why a factory representative of Kaiser Aluminum and Chemical Company stopped by for a visit one day. He was interested in locating a distributor for a new Kaiser conductor development, aluminum triplex. He personally handled the big investor-owned electric utilities, but he needed a distributor to introduce the new triplex to the public power utilities in the area.

Before the new triplex was available on the market, it was necessary to run three individual copper wires from a cross-arm on the power pole to a building being served power. Aluminum triplex consisted of three insulated stranded aluminum conductors twisted together into a sort of cable that could be strung between a power pole and a building being served.

The advantages of the triplex included lower cost and enhanced appearance. One disadvantage was that the aluminum conductors in the triplex and the copper conductors in the building, when together, could corrode and fail if not connected properly.

"Well, Bill, do you suppose your general office would consider introducing and warehousing our conductor in the Oregon district?" the Kaiser man asked.

"That is a decision I can make for this district," I said. "You bet we can do a good job at introducing your product to the public power companies, and are ready to go as soon as we sign the papers."

It did not take very long for our customers to see the advantages of triplex. We welcomed the substantial increase in sales volume. The Kaiser people who contacted us were outstanding. We were invited to their manufacturing plant in California, and to attend various product meetings. We were able to extend our distributor arrangement to our Seattle office, and a year or two later, after observing our excellent sales volume and earnings, our general office arranged for San Francisco too to sell Kaiser triplex.

Perhaps we should clarify the function of Maydwell & Hartzell in the sales business. Were we manufacturers' representatives, or were we sales engineers, or perhaps distributors? We were a bit of all three. We directly represented the factories of Kearney, Kortick, Victor, and a few other manufacturers as their agent in our sales area.

Rather than sell the products of our manufacturers to electrical distributor companies for their warehouse stocks, we chose to take our manufacturers' products into our own warehouses. Then, as sales engineers, we sold to our electric utility customers, large and small, either by direct factory shipment or out of our warehouse stocks. Wearing our distributor hats, we were called on regularly by factory representatives of the larger manufacturers we represented, like Allis-Chalmers. This role as customers of large manufacturers gave us an opportunity to observe the big company reps' methods, and to evaluate their effectiveness.

Regardless of which hat we were wearing, the very functional part of working as a sales engineer was extremely rewarding and challenging—a fun career where hard work nearly always paid off, one way or another. That being said, not everyone could function as a sales engineer or a factory rep, and big companies seem to have some reps of both types.

In my packaged substation business activity at M&H, Sandy Sandelin, an Allis-Chalmers factory sales rep, supplied me with power transformers, voltage regulators and other very expensive pieces of equipment. Then there was Bob Gilton, at that time a factory engineer specializing in the Allis-Chalmers voltage regulators. Both Bob and Sandy were outstanding as engineers and fun to be with.

Bob Weaver, regional manager of Allis-Chalmers, was another example of a top-rated factory sales rep. Bob had a disarming Texas drawl and was fun to be with, lots of laughs, but he also was an expert in his product line and a sharp businessman. Bob always had three complete bids ready to submit, signed and ready, stowed away in his folder. Just before the bid deadline, he would pull one of the bids out and present it. He knew which one had the best chance. More often than not, we were awarded the business.

12

Exit as Regional Manager

The game of golf has been important to me throughout my career, not only as a healthy, active outdoor sport, but also as a means of getting to know many interesting people. Rather than dealing in business with a casual acquaintance on a regular basis, we would break the ice with a few rounds of golf, allowing a more or less free exchange of ideas and opinions.

During my years at WISCO building ships, golf was a means of getting away from the office for a few hours during the week. The pressure on those of us heading departments got to be pretty severe at times, and a game of golf seemed to remove the job and its problems from our minds for a while. A person could not play decent golf without concentrating on the game, so job problems were set aside.

All of us were on the job seven days a week, and we looked forward from one week to the next to our afternoon of golf. None of us were real hot golfers, but we did relax and have fun.

Winter golf was great. If there was no snow, we would play even in the freezing cold. We took turns furnishing a jug of liquor that fit nicely in a golf bag pocket. We would play the game of "sip or smell." The rules were very uncomplicated. If we all shot the same score on a hole, nothing happened. However, if someone won, it meant there were one or more losers, and the winner was privileged to take a sip out of the jug, after which the losers, in turn, would each take only a smell. This game kept us warm. Also, the loser on the first nine holes had a good chance to be a winner on the last nine.

In my career as sales engineer and district manager at Maydwell & Hartzell, golf became an even more important part of my contact with customers. For years my Thursday afternoon foursome consisted of me and three officials from one investor-owned electric company, and the other members of my early Saturday morning foursome were from a different investor-owned electric company.

One of the executives in the Thursday group would keep the conversation lively by telling us about his experiences as a young man in Alaska, where he played the piano in a house of ill repute to make money for room and board. He would sing a song or two from those days if his game was okay. Our foursome played for dimes. The game was Bingle, Bangle, Bungle.

The Bingle winner on each fairway was the player who first landed his ball on the green. He won a dime from each of the other three. The Bangle winner was the player who landed on the green closest to the pin, good for a dime, and the Bungle winner—for a dime—was the first one in the cup. Each winner was carefully noted on our scorecards. The rivalry was intense. Accusations of cheating, lack of ethics, violation of PGA rules, and so on, would start on the first fairway and continue even after the game, via shouts in the shower room.

Road trips in good weather always included golf clubs in the trunk. In Longview, Washington, I could always count on Cecil Wise, the superintendent, for a game after work. A trip down the Oregon coast always included a stop at Newport, and a round of golf after work with manager Harold Sudduth and engineer John Schriner.

Heading over the mountains east to Redmond, Oregon, a golf game with John Norlin, the manager, was quite iffy. The problem was getting John out of the office in time to play a round. He could not leave until all pending business was cleared away.

John was a very personable, friendly man. We first met in the early 1950s, soon after my assignment to M&H Portland District. Central Electric's power distribution lines were widely spread over many miles of mostly sagebrush desert, with few farms in widely scattered areas, typical of many electric cooperatives at the time. I considered John tops among all the electric cooperative managers I contacted. None of them were sub-par; most were friendly and efficient; but John went one step further.

He made it a point to know all his employees—office help and linemen—and visited with some of them every day. He used to say his people did their best every day to make him look good as manager. The employees' high regard for John really showed. The office atmosphere was casual but very efficient. Sometimes I would find him out in the territory visiting with a line crew who were setting a power pole or changing out a transformer. At other times I would find him visiting with a rancher who wanted a power line extension.

By the time John retired, he had built a campus-style service center. The city of Redmond had built a busy airport, modern shops and restaurants, supermarkets, and industrial park, and an improved golf course. Perhaps we should not credit John with all the growth in his district during the past four decades, but we all knew his foresight, planning, and managerial skills had a lot to do with providing the foundation for growth with adequate electric power.

In addition to golf games with customers, business lunches were almost a daily event. My principal reason for arranging a business lunch was to get the utility person out of the office and away from the pressure of the telephone and distractions from other employees, so that we could discuss in a relaxed atmosphere his concerns in regard to the subject at hand. Also, in my crowded schedule, it allowed me to accomplish much more constructive exchanges of thought with the customer than I could in a busy office setting.

Golf games and lunches were certainly part of my job as a sales engineer. During a golf game, business was seldom discussed, though it might be mentioned during refreshments after the game. Both golf and lunches were excellent ways to become better acquainted with customers. I knew that if we developed a relationship based on mutual trust and respect, my customer would see to it that my company would receive a fair shake when it came to handing out business.

Meanwhile, back at my job as M&H district manager, changes were taking place. Laurel had taken over from Mary and was doing very well. The office routine was back to normal, but only for a few weeks. Ed Reichwein, district manager at the Seattle office and my old friend and ex-employee, suddenly gave notice he would resign in thirty days to take a position with a larger company. Our general office asked me to look for a replacement. The first person to come to mind was my salesman, Hugh Dewar.

Hugh and I had a long talk. Neither of us was very anxious to break up our team and uproot Hugh and his family to Seattle. However, after a few days, Hugh decided to give it a try. We arranged for his transfer to Seattle.

George McMurdo, our warehouseman, was anxious to try sales. He had good product knowledge and an amiable personality, and he was a loyal, hard worker, so we transferred him into Hugh's job.

Hugh had included among his Oregon customers the contractors who built high voltage transmission lines. Bonneville Power and other utilities issued invitations to bid to the line contractors from time to time for their major construction contracts. The contractors then asked suppliers for bids for whatever material was required. The big dollars were in aluminum conductor. Our bid was always to furnish Kaiser aluminum conductor. Most of the time we lost out to a competitor, Reynolds Metals. Reynolds had a factory sales rep named Joe Shelley, who managed, one way or another, to "eat our lunch" on the big jobs.

The first big line job bid that came up after Hugh left was up to me to handle. The bid was out of town, requiring an overnight stay at a small hotel. I walked into the lounge for a cocktail at the bar before dinner. Joe Shelley was sitting there. The stool next to Joe was vacant, so I sat down, ordered a cocktail, and started to visit with him.

We continued our visit during dinner. Our service in World War II came up for discussion. Joe had served in the Navy on an aircraft carrier, which sank in the South Pacific, and he ended up in the water for some time before being rescued. The aircraft carrier he served on was the USS *Wasp,* the same aircraft carrier I had worked on at the Bethlehem Steel Fore River shipyard. I told Joe about the "blood ship" conversation I had with the old timer during the launching of the *Wasp* after two Naval Reserve planes collided in midair at its launching, killing the pilots.

From that evening on, Joe and I became good friends. He later left Reynolds, worked for me for several months, and finally had his own rewarding career as manager of Oregon's Electrical Contractors Bid Depository.

On top of all the personnel changes, my job title changed from Portland district manager to Northwest regional manager. My office was to remain in Portland, where I would also run the Portland District, but in addition I would supervise operations in Washington and a new office opening in Montana. All of this added extra travel and new people to train, with very little adjustment in salary.

It would be unfair to accept the promotion and leave in a few months, as I would be doing, because my fortieth birthday was fast approaching, signaling my self-imposed deadline for starting my company.

It was late November of 1957 when I wrote to Pop Hartzell advising him of my decision to resign as of January 1, 1958, and to stay on if requested until February 1 to help my successor take over. After receiving my letter, Pop called, asking me to visit with him at his home.

We had a comfortable visit, relaxed over cocktails, and talked far into the night. We discussed my plans in detail. As far as starting the new company was concerned, Pop argued the timing was not good. The country was in a slight recession. Banks were restrictive on new loans. Good arguments, but I was determined to get under way on my own. The next morning I agreed to stay on until March 1 to help locate and train a replacement, and to check out with factories we represented.

During my remaining time, Pop was agreeable to my taking some of the initial steps in forming my company. I assured Pop I would respect his interests and would not compete directly with M&H, and that my ultimate objective was to manufacture.

My career as a manufacturer's rep extended from January 1949 to December 1957. I had carefully selected this short career to prepare me to build my own company, to serve the industry of my choice.

I can highly recommend a career as a factory sales rep to anyone willing to work and learn. The lifestyle is rewarding in many ways for those interested in a lifetime sales career. It was certainly a major factor in the success of my own company.

13

Time to Start Western Power Products, Inc.

Since early 1955, I had targeted 1957 as my final year with M&H. My neighbor, Bob McFarlane, was a CPA. We had many discussions about my plans to start a business. Bob gave me lots of good advice, and now and then a case study of another entrepreneur going broke and why, or of someone making it big and why.

My banker friend, Virgil Solso, had known of my plans since 1955. He had a lot of financial advice. One valuable suggestion was to establish a line of credit with a bank early on, many months before starting a business. Once the business was under way, if we might need several thousand dollars temporarily, the loan committee at the bank should have a loan file on me showing my credit to be good. Virgil kept reminding me to apply for short-term loans to pay for my major personal bills and to repay the loans ahead of schedule to establish my credit.

The first order of business after meeting with Pop was to visit the corporation commissioner's office in Salem, the state capital, to pick up the necessary registration forms and to check the procedures for registering a corporate name. The clerk advised me to make out the form carefully, and to list three preferences for a corporate name. The names would be checked for duplication or possible confusion with other companies authorized to do business in Oregon.

The next thing to do was to find an inexpensive office and to establish a name, address, and telephone number—a place to get started. Here is where another neighbor was helpful. He was a retired carpenter who had purchased an old commercial structure at Sylvan, a few miles west of Portland, and divided the space into offices. He offered me an office for thirty-five dollars a month. The rent included a receptionist at the front door who would take my calls when I was away.

In mid-December, I called my friend Jim Kearney, Jr., president of the James R. Kearney Corporation, and told him of my plans to leave M&H. He asked me to come to St. Louis to kick around some ideas. This suggestion sounded good to me. I would take the train, traveling in a roomette, which would give me a few days alone to plan my next steps, and to come up with three choices for a company name.

The visit with Jim and his staff went well. A Kearney sales territory in the Southwest was offered to me if I would reconsider my career goals and continue as a sales engineer.

"Gosh, Jim, I sure appreciate your offer of a really choice territory in a growth area, but it's important to me to give my plans a go. I will keep in touch, and if my business does not develop within a reasonable time, I will get back to you." Jim was a straight shooter and a good friend.

On the train ride home, I decided the name Western Power Products, Inc. seemed to be a good fit for what we would be trying to do, so that became my number one choice. After my arrival, I checked out the Sylvan office space. At about ten by fifteen feet, it wasn't too roomy, but there was space enough for a desk, chair, file cabinet, and drafting table.

There was a need to file promptly with the corporation officer. Because of my agreement with Pop to continue as the regional manager through March, I asked an attorney friend, Dave Brewer, to file for me and show the organizers as Virgil Solso, president, and Eugene Compton, an insurance agent, as secretary-treasurer.

1. Roommates Harry Stone, Bill Wild, and Dave Williams in Sacramento, California.

2. Ship launching, Bethlehem Steel, San Francisco.

3. Fog bowl insulators installed near Newport, Oregon.

5. Mrs. Mary Olson, the author's daughter, with the fuse link storage can.

4. A rural electric power distribution substation.

6. John Chichester demonstrating the hand line block.

7. Mirisol Verdusco with the rope block.

8. The LW-100 tension brake in use by PGE in Salem, Oregon.

9. Bob Foster with the LW-100 tension brake.

10. Wheel chock installed under truck wheel.

11. Factory crew demonstrates the strength of the fiberglass enclosure.

12. A Western Suburban substation.

13. Western Power Products plant, Hood River, Oregon.

14. Mrs. Joan R. Bright at the computer.

15. John Chichester demonstrates the switching power pedestal.

16. Western Power Products management team (left to right): Bill Bright, Lynn Beier, Jim Coon, Larry Sanguras.

17. At the completion of the sale of Western Power Products (left to right): Jim Zboyovsky, President, Kearney National, of Atlanta, Georgia; Don McEwen, attorney, McEwen, Gisvold, Rankin, of Portland, Oregon; Bill Bright, President, Western Power Products, Inc., of Hood River, Oregon.

We were required to pay $1,000 for issuance of shares, and we asked for authority to issue two hundred shares at $50 per share par value in common stock. The shares would be held in our treasury account for future sale to employees.

As a result, the Articles of Incorporation, filed January 9, 1958, authorized Western Power Products to "buy, sell, distribute, or otherwise deal in, at wholesale or retail, capital goods and other products used in the power industries, extractive industries and allied fields."

Now that we had a company name, a business address, and a phone number, the next items on my to-do list were setting up a corporate bank account, applying for a city business license, ordering calling cards, and selecting a company automobile. With all of the basic company chores taken care of, I started looking in earnest for things to sell to electric utilities. At the same time, I continued to take care of M&H business through March 31. To hit the ground running with Western Power Products meant I had to make sales in April.

To finish the corporate organization, we met at attorney Dave Brewer's office to discuss and adopt corporation by-laws and to make Brewer the president, Solso vice president, and Bob McFarlane secretary-treasurer. We also voted to employ me as manager, giving me full authority for all contracts and purchases. We also voted to award Brewer four shares of stock for his services as our attorney—this in lieu of cash.

All this allowed the corporation to be legal and functional for the several weeks more that I was to be involved with M&H. Later, in June, Brewer resigned as president, and McFarlane resigned as secretary-treasurer. I was elected president and McFarlane treasurer. Brewer was elected secretary. We designated Virgil's bank, Citizen's Bank of Lake Oswego, as our bank, and voted to pay me a salary of $650 dollars per month plus expenses.

At the entrepreneur entry stage, it was particularly important to have a CPA, a banker, and an attorney to guide me—not just any professionals, but people I knew and trusted. If I would have enough sense to ask questions of my advisors, and if I followed this trusted advice, my chances of success would be greatly enhanced.

Incidentally, in selling or issuing shares of my company stock, it was very important for me as founder to retain in my name more than 50 percent of the total shares of stock issued, in order to retain voting control of the corporation. It was not the number of shares in the company's treasury that determined control of the company; rather, control was determined by the person(s) who owned the majority of the shares issued.

Early in the first spring, we became aware of a substation packaging job at one of the electric cooperatives, which would be out for bids soon. When I left M&H, they chose to get out of the substation business, so here was business I could go after under my agreement with Pop Hartzell.

Since I could no longer go to Kearney as a source of switches, because their contract was with M&H, I dropped by the office of a local switch manufacturer, Schwager-Wood Corporation, to see if I could pick up their catalog. The owners were both men highly regarded in the electric utility industry. Gus Schwager, of Swiss parentage, was a brilliant design engineer. Max Wood, affable and outgoing, took care of marketing. Their new plant was on the outskirts of Portland.

We met in the morning, had lunch, and talked all afternoon. In the evening we had cocktails at Max's home. Max not only set us up to purchase their switches with an original equipment manufacturer (OEM) discount for substation activity, but also made their entire product line available to me to sell to public power companies, and extended us a distributor discount.

This was great news. I could distribute their catalog to my customers with my business card attached. Within one week I was receiving orders. The deal with Max included open account billing at my request. The customer's purchase order would come to my office. We would then place our purchase order on Schwager-Wood, with instruction to ship direct to the customers. Schwager-Wood would then invoice us, and we were to pay them within their thirty-day term period.

Then we would invoice our customer at the published catalog price, which would be ten percent higher than our cost. The high voltage switches cost hundreds or thousands of dollars, so ten percent margin looked good. The billing procedure may seem involved, but it was a routine to benefit the manufacturer, the distributor, and the customer.

This was a situation where good banking connections were important. We had to pay the factory within their thirty-day period from date of invoice. We couldn't receive payment from our customer in time to get our payment to the factory within thirty days, so we took a copy of the invoice we had sent to our customer, to our bank for security. The bank lent us enough money to pay the factory within their terms, and when we received the check from our customer, we deposited it in the bank and paid the bank a small fee covering interest on the amount borrowed for a week or two. This invoice financing transaction also looked involved but became a series of routines. Without a good credit rating, a manufacturer or a distributor could not function for very long.

Shortly after the Schwager-Wood visit, I stopped in to visit Sam Lee, president of Schmitt Steel. We had become well acquainted in the previous several years, since Sam supplied the steel structure for our packaged substations. Sam and I discussed my new status, and the fact that M&H would not be in the substation business in the future. The problem was that the M&H sales manager hated substations with a passion. They were much too complicated for him to understand, even though we reps sold lots of our manufacturers' products in our substations.

However, Western Power Products would definitely be in the substation business. We wanted to continue trading with Schmitt Steel and wanted to continue buying structure on open account. Also, I wanted to buy certain hardware items used in pole line construction. I offered to work with Sam's employees to develop a list of pole line specialties for us to sell.

Sam offered to provide office space for us in his building at the same rent as we were paying at Sylvan. A large portion of the daylight basement was vacant. He would have a new ceiling installed and new paint. The space was about twenty by forty feet.

We had a deal. We had another product line to sell and could continue with our substation work. We moved into the Schmitt Steel building and held a board meeting there on December 11.

There's another advantage of serving the industry as a factory rep before starting your own company. If you establish a reputation as a successful factory rep, other manufacturers will be eager to sign you on—thus providing you the opportunity for building important cash flow to finance your operations.

In the weeks following my negotiations with Sam Lee, we had a large bid for a packaged substation coming up. We needed a factory quotation for a large power transformer, a voltage regulator, and an oil circuit breaker. These were big-ticket items—major power plant equipment components that we had previously purchased from Allis-Chalmers through their Portland factory sales rep, Sandy Sandelin. In the past, I had the M&H credit rating to back me up on open account purchases, but no more. With Western Power Products' minimal credit line, I did not know if Sandy would even talk to me.

My phone call to Sandy went along fine, though. He took down all the details of my inquiry, and then suggested we have lunch the following day at the Multnomah Athletic Club, where we both were members. I was still thinking that Sandy would turn down my inquiry, due to my company's lack of a credit line.

We met for lunch, and Sandy never once mentioned credit. What he wanted to talk about was a new Allis-Chalmers policy to assign manufacturers' (factory) reps to cover public power utilities in all areas around the U.S. and to limit their field sales employees, like Sandy, to coverage of the large investor-owned utilities. The Oregon/Southern Washington territory had not been assigned, although a number of large distributor companies were pressing Sandy for the assignment.

"Say, Bill, would you be interested in taking this territory?" Sandy asked.

"I am looking for a major line, Sandy, and I would be thrilled to represent one of the best in the business," I replied.

The big three manufacturers of major high voltage compo-nents in the U.S. were General Electric, Westinghouse, and Allis-

Chalmers. The last was famous for its design of voltage regulators, both pole-mounted and substation types.

A voltage regulator resembles a distribution transformer in appearance—a circular steel tank with porcelain insulators on top. As the name implies, an internal mechanism maintains the voltage in the power distribution system to fixed levels, for example plus or minus 2 percent. This is necessary for the efficient operation of household appliances and other electrical equipment.

Sandy recorded all our WPP information needed to make out his agent application to their headquarters in Milwaukie, Wisconsin. He would keep me advised. Later we were appointed the Allis-Chalmers agent for the Oregon territory. No other product line could have helped us more at that time.

What gave us the nod over the well-established large distributors? The fact that we had been active in the packaged substation business was, I believe, the major reason, along with the fact that I enjoyed a good reputation among our utility customers. Thanks again to Bruce Shavere for getting me started in the substation business.

Part of the deal with Allis-Chalmers was the necessity for me to attend their first meeting for national agents. The meeting was held at their West Allis factory, located about six miles west of downtown Milwaukee, Wisconsin. The two-day meeting of about forty agents was interesting and informative. In addition to establishing personal relationships with their factory personnel, getting acquainted with successful agents from other parts of the U. S. was also very interesting and useful to me in future years.

Western Power Products could then advertise the fact that we were the exclusive public power distributor-agent for Schwager-Wood switches, Schmitt Steel structures, and Allis-Chalmers power equipment. We could compete with anyone in the Northwest for packaged substations. We also had great sales potential for routine sales of voltage regulators, transformers and high voltage disconnect switches. All this happened in our first year of business.

The first-year goal of establishing a positive cash flow had been accomplished. The only thing that made this critical achievement possible was my previous record as a district manager for

M&H. As it worked out, I did not solicit any of the three key product lines to sell as a distributor but was able to qualify only on the basis of experience and reputation. I was moving up on my career objective: not to make a million dollars, but to build a profitable manufacturing/marketing business.

My next meeting with my old buddy and career partner, Bill Wild, found him still much involved in the ship repair business, and talking about the prospects of moving their ship repair operations to San Diego.

"Okay, why move to San Diego? Why not join me in Western Power Products?" I asked. I told Bill of our rapid progress in completing agency agreements with three quality manufacturers, and noted that cash flow was sufficient to pay expenses for both of us as we built the company.

Bill replied that he felt comfortable about the future, staying with his ship repair career. There was talk about a title of vice president for him in the near future. And so, doing what he enjoyed for a sound company, with a promise of vice president status, was exactly the goal he envisioned years earlier, during our career planning. We both planned our work and worked our plan toward different career goals.

"How come you were able to make deals to represent those manufacturers? Don't they have their own salesmen?" Bill asked.

"I've spent several years working as a sales engineer, contacting people in the electric utility industry. These manufacturers knew about my success in building up Maydwell & Hartzell in Oregon as well as our success in the substation business. So perhaps my record qualified me in product knowledge and personal contact among the utilities. Besides, they all know I'm starting my own business, and will work real hard to make it successful," I said.

With the move to the Schmitt Steel building, and the addition of the Allis-Chalmers and Schwager-Wood product lines, I now needed office help. The paperwork and telephone calls were building fast, and I could not afford to be tied down in an office. After a search I hired John Benedetti as office manager. John had recently graduated from the University of Portland. Arriving for the job interview, he zoomed into the parking lot a few feet from the entrance door, driving a racy rag-top roadster. John was a very intelligent, quiet, personable young man, and had all the skills I was interested in. He was single, but seriously interested in a young lady undergraduate.

John fit in well from the first day. He took over and ran the inside operations, handled telephone and written quotations, prepared monthly cash flow/operating statements. In short, he soon was as important to me as my right arm.

We also needed sales help to give proper coverage around the state for our principals. About that time my old friend Joe Shelley dropped by the office. Joe had been a crack salesman for Reynolds Aluminum but had left them and was looking around. We made a deal, and Joe came to work for us. Now the company boasted three employees: Bill, Joe and John.

With John and Joe aboard, there would be more time now for me to further develop the substation business, which included a lot of night work detailing substation arrangements on the drafting board. It also allowed time for product development.

My long-term objective was to develop our own line of products, while giving all necessary time to the needs of our customers and the factories whom we were representing, and who were providing us with steady cash flow.

14

Underway with New Product Development

When making long-term plans involving product development, manufacturing, and marketing, it was also certainly prudent to give high priority to enlisting a professional team to service the company in advertising, insurance, and patent law. Just as the professional team mentioned earlier, of attorney, accountant and banker—friends who became knowledgeable contributors to the success of the company—were outstanding in their fields, so were the people who provided the professional know-how in advertising, insurance, and patent law. We were fortunate to engage the services of three of the best.

About the time that John Benedetti joined us, we needed a small brochure put together describing our Schmitt Steel pole line hardware, as well as some of Pacific Light Metal Foundry products. The brochure, to be handed out to our customers, would identify Western Power Products as their source. Bob Miller recommended the advertising firm of Westerman-Webber, a small firm with a fine reputation.

I arranged a visit with Ken Webber, and brought along sketches and support data describing what I thought would tell our story. Ken went over everything carefully and took over from there.

Ken called several times on the phone with questions about application of our products to clarify details. Within ten days, he put together a very professional-looking, easy-to-read, attractive brochure, all within his estimates of time and cost.

As time went on and our company grew, our product catalog requirements and periodic pricelist changes increased. We required national magazine ads and miscellaneous news releases, and it all grew as we grew. Ken soon knew as much about our products, company policy, and marketing approach as we did. He became a sort of staff officer who ruled our advertising activity, always making sure we received the most for our advertising dollar. We eventually budgeted 5 to 7 percent of our gross sales to advertising, and Ken took care of it all.

One of Ken's money-saving services involved new products that we developed from time to time. He would send a photo and write-up of a product to a popular trade magazine, which would then print it free of charge as a news item. This process generated lots of inquiries from potential customers and resulted in good initial product sales, time after time. Ken and his wife, Gloria, a widely acclaimed watercolor artist, became close family friends as well as valued business associates.

Another important service area was product liability insurance, and the balance between premium cost and the degree of exposure. Product liability was out there, for example, and multiplied every time we furnished an additional packaged substation.

The risk to utility personnel and to the public exposed to injury by high voltage accidents caused many problems for the insurance companies. It was up to our insurance broker to allay the fears of the insurance company so that we could obtain an annual policy at reasonable cost.

The insurance firm of Campbell, Galt, and Newlands, had a good reputation around town, so I called on Tom Galt shortly after getting Western Power Products under way, and went over our business activity with him. Tom approached our account much like Ken Webber approached our advertising. He had to know all about our products and our market. Here again, we had a fine multi-year relationship. Tom coached us thoroughly on the use of warning labels regarding the application of our products. He also strongly recommended thorough test procedures for all products before shipment, recorded by serial numbers. The fact that we never suffered a loss (although we had a few threatening lawsuits) despite our widespread exposure all over the country in the use of our high voltage tools, products, and equipment, says quite a lot about Tom's guidance.

The years I spent serving in the industry as a factory rep were extremely valuable as background in product development. This was key to developing patentable products to produce and market as an entrepreneur. Following are some examples.

It was early in 1959 when we started to move into our own products. One of the buyers at Pacific Power & Light mentioned that they were looking for a source of fuse link storage cans. The large manufacturer who had been furnishing them for years had discontinued the product line.

"Would your company know of a source for these cans?" he said as he handed me the sample.

"Well, Al, not right off hand, but I may be able to find you a source if I could borrow the sample and check our suppliers," I said.

"Okay, it's yours for a week. We use them regularly, order them in quantities of five hundred," he said.

To explain the function of a fuse link storage can, I told Al that utilities try to protect primary power lines from complete loss of power caused by a local accident, such as a branch falling across power lines or a car hitting a power pole. They accomplished this by isolating the section of power line where the accident occurs, utilizing fused disconnect switches. The current capacity of the fuses in the switches becomes progressively less starting from the power source on down the power line, so it is important that a properly rated fuse be installed in a switch when replacing one that has melted and disconnected the faulted power line. To be sure the lineman used the proper size of fuse at each switch for replacements, a storage can holding several fuses was installed near the switches at the pole top.

The fuse containers then in use were made of aluminum tubing about four inches in diameter and ten inches long, fitted with a steel hanger to bolt it to the power pole. The container had a removable aluminum cap, and was welded in watertight heavy-duty construction, much too rugged and expensive to manufacture.

With some brainstorming, we developed a better fuse link storage container (Plate 5). We eliminated welding by using a metal spinning process. A false bottom with drain hole would eliminate condensation, and a plastic cap attached with a cord, along with an improved pole-mounting bracket, completed the new design. We could sell it to the utility for less than they had been paying, and still make a good profit. The customer was delighted and ordered the first five hundred, with many thousands to follow. Rather than farm the job out, I ordered the parts from two different shops. If I ordered the complete container from one shop, they could become competitors.

Since we had no shop at this point, assembly, packaging, and shipping were scheduled for my two-car garage. To accomplish this first product production, I hired our first shop employee—Mary A. Bright, a blonde eight-year old—and my daughter. We negotiated a salary of ten cents per hour, plus all the food she could eat. By standing on a wooden box, she was able to reach the workbench. Then she would assemble the parts, install the rivets, and I would pean the rivets, and clean and pack the finished parts. I delivered the early orders to the power company warehouse, always in time to have coffee with the crew.

I had one problem with my shop employee—she insisted on being paid every evening at the end of the shift. Then she promptly deposited her entire day's pay in her bank. After growing up, Mary developed and managed our cost accounting department. When pressed for details about her part in the early days of Western Power Products, she told people she remembered well the good food after working with her dad in the garage, but has no recollection at all of ever being paid any money.

Mentioning cost accounting in a manufacturing business reminds me that it was of the utmost importance that management knew exactly the percentage of which category of cost was included in the total reported cost of each product in production. Otherwise the company had no basis on which to assign profit margins in sales prices. Without accurate and meaningful profit margins, companies went broke. Monitoring and reporting accurate costs of multiple products being produced required a cost accountant with the mental discipline of an infantry drill sergeant.

Everyone involved in production had to make an accurate report of labor, time, and material costs every day. Mary grew up with the expertise to handle that most important department with a skillful combination of pleasant encouragement to those working in production to make their accurate timely reports, but all hell would break loose for anyone caught filing inaccurate reports.

It has been reported that a large percentage of companies that go broke were not aware of their true costs of operation.

Although our garage worked fine for assembly of fuse link storage cans, I knew that we really needed a low-cost shop space for light manufacturing and assembly. Joe Shelley suggested that his brother-in-law Skip had warehouse space available and might make us a deal.

Skip was more than willing. We erected a barrier to separate Skip's end of the warehouse from our end and built a long workbench. We purchased the few tools needed and were all set up with our first shop. Here we established a precedent we followed in setting up future shops. We paid no money for electrical, carpentry, or paint work. We did it all ourselves and actually enjoyed the experience of working together to build something worthwhile.

Our next product development project came to light one day during a lunch with Bob Miller, president of Pacific Light Metals Foundry. Bob and I tried to have lunch together once a month to discuss various business subjects. Bob was an interesting, informative, friendly person.

Bob's distributor in California had shipped him a steel lineman's hand line block, asking if Bob could make it in magnesium, because the steel block was awkward for the lineman to use. Bob said he could reduce the weight by one-half, which he proceeded to do. The California customer liked the lighter block and started ordering them in good quantities.

"Hey, if you can sell this block here in the Northwest, you're welcome to it," Bob said.

Some people would call a rope block a "pulley." A hand line was a one-half-inch diameter rope that extended from the ground up the power pole to where a lineman was working, then ran through the rope block and back down to the ground. If the lineman needed a tool or material, he yelled down to the ground man. The ground man placed the tool in a canvas bucket, which was attached to one end of the hand line, then pulled on the other end to raise the bucket up to the lineman. The ground man had to be careful to steer the bucket away from obstructions as it moved up the pole.

Bob gave me the magnesium hand line block for a sample. It was lightweight, and I could see several areas where the design could be improved. Perhaps this hand line block would be a new product design and development product, a niche for us to exploit. The first step would be to learn all I could about hand line blocks. The best place to find out what was good or bad about a tool was to talk with the people who used them every day, and to the utility safety departments who were interested in protecting the linemen from injury.

Regarding design, the first thing obvious to me was the advantage of a lightweight rope block. To get the block to the pole top, the lineman had to hook the block and handline on his belt while climbing the pole, so saving a couple of pounds was important to him.

I learned that the steel or wood shell rope blocks they were using were general-use, industrial-type rope blocks. They complained about the sharp edges of the rope sheave, which caused their hand lines to fray, thus collecting dust and moisture that made the rope conductive after time, which was bad news around high voltage. Sometimes the top fittings or sheave would fall apart while raising a bucket up the pole, causing the bucket to fall to the ground and injure the ground man.

The safety engineers in the investor-owned utilities all had records of multiple cases of lineman injuries caused by block failures. Therefore, the entire block needed to be redesigned so that it could not come apart in use, and it needed to be rated for "safe working load" just as rope blocks were rated for industrial use.

I traveled for a month around Oregon making the rounds of my utility customers, doing my usual business, but also carrying with me the sample handline block. I made it a point to stop in to see safety department people and line crews, and seldom did I visit a line crew or safety engineer who did not have an opinion of what the ideal handline block should be.

Practically every one of the dozens of individuals I consulted seemed to appreciate the fact that I was seeking their professional advice. Most, however, seemed to think nothing would come of their suggestions.

After gathering all the design opinions, we began to visualize what the ideal handline block would look like. We also began to realize the potential market for the ideal block, designed just for linemen, and it was in the hundreds of thousands. This could be an exciting project, well worth the time and effort it would take to develop.

This was a project for my light metals expert Bob Miller to become involved with. We held the first of a dozen meetings where function and design were discussed. Bob had to know load figures in order to design the proper sectional thickness of metal throughout the block. In order to keep the size, weight, and cost of the hand line block to the minimum, I felt the strength rating should reflect the recommended application of the block.

The block was to be designed for use with a lineman's handline. A "handline" meant the strain applied to the rope was to be by people, not by an engine-driven winch. So, if only humans would be pulling on the line, I could see no more than two men, each weighing up to 250 pounds, applying their combined weight simultaneously to one end of the line, or 500 pounds of strain maximum.

The 500 pounds of strain on one end of the line could lift a load of something under 500 pounds, which would place a combined load on the top fittings of the block of 1,000 pounds. Therefore, we could designate the safe working load as 1,000 pounds, and the design ultimate load, where failure could occur, as 3,000 pounds. We should set our factory test load to apply to each block before shipment at 2,000 pounds. Also, we would cast into the surface of the cheeks of the blocks the 1,000-pound safe working load designation. Some of my thinking in setting these standards was no doubt influenced by the advice of my insurance consultant, Tom Galt.

Bob designed the block castings in an aircraft alloy of magnesium for maximum strength and minimum weight. A three-inch diameter aluminum sheave would be grooved for the half-inch manila rope, and inset into the side castings just enough to prevent the sheave rims from coming into contact with the hand lines.

Shielding the rims of the rope sheave took care of a major gripe of the linemen. Another major gripe was that the nuts that secured the sheave axle tended to come loose, allowing the block to fail. We solved that problem by recessing the nuts into the side castings, making it impossible for the nuts to turn after assembly.

All the parts went together as planned. The tensile tests again proved Bob's mastery of light metal design. Failure occurred in the area of 4,000-pound tensile test load.

One other design problem remained. The linemen wanted the top fitting fixed so it could swing open to place their hand line into the sheave, rather than threading it in, since the hand lines had fittings on both ends. No problem.

The handline block (Plate 6) was presented to a few of our customers, and it was a hit from the beginning. We set up our small shop to do as much of the manufacturing as was economically feasible. We received castings from Bob and did all the finishing work, drilling, and grinding. The axles required special machine work, so we farmed them out. Various other shop operations were required before final assembly and painting. The axle, the sheave design turning on ball bearings, the axle nuts recessed into the side castings, and the lightweight, handy shape were all real grabbers with the linemen. The handline block development project underscored the value of having our own shop to fine-tune a new product.

Now that we had a new product approved by local utilities, the next step was to market the handline block. This involved preparing descriptive literature with photos and full specifications—information necessary for our customers' files. With literature available, the next step in introducing a new product was to show it to the people you would like to see using it. I loaded a couple dozen blocks into the trunk of my car and visited the giant investor-owned electric utilities in San Francisco, Los Angeles, and San Diego. They all had favorable opinions of the block and all promised to forward the samples I left to their various departments involved in the standards approval process.

The last day of my introductory trip was spent with the Los Angeles Department of Water and Power, a giant utility. My first contacts were with the purchasing department. They directed me to a series of offices and departments, all in turn directing me to higher authority. By late afternoon I was told that a Mr. Lawther, the general superintendent, would have the say on approval of the block. When I arrived at his office at 4:30 P.M., his secretary told me to stand by; Lawther would have ten minutes for me before leaving at 5:00.

In his office I gave him a sample of the block, and we discussed its features in detail. He had been very close to line crews during his career and knew exactly what we were doing in our design and why. He was a rare blend of practical line construction know-how and forceful administrative skill. In no time at all it was 6:30. I left him some blocks, literature, and a verbal price estimate.

"If all goes well, I want to equip our entire crew of nine hundred linemen with your blocks. However, everything purchased in this utility is by public bid. We'll buy them one hundred at a time," he said.

True to his word, their bid specs were issued, detailing all of our features. We were the only company who could meet the specifications. We kept track of our shipments to them for a few years, and quantities shipped far exceeded the nine hundred estimate. Perhaps some were used for projects other than line work.

Bob's production process did not lend itself to producing large quantities of small parts, such as our block parts. Also, warping in the castings during the heat treat process made it impossible to interchange parts, so as sales volume started to take off, we were forced to find an alternate source for our castings. We had a major local manufacturer who produced aluminum castings for Boeing Aircraft and others, using the injection mold process, so I decided to review our hand line block with them to see whether their process would resolve our production problems.

Injection molding is a process whereby massive steel die blocks in mated pairs are machined out in the shape of each part to be produced. All of the handline block castings parts were included in the same die, called a family die. The parts were produced to extremely exact tolerances, so that all parts were interchangeable. If true, injection molded parts would reduce our assembly time by 90 percent, and reduce our molded parts costs by 50 percent. The company engineers promised their castings would maintain our rated strength and weight standards.

The finished castings had a much improved appearance, with our company name and catalog number in raised letters. The die, which we would be required to pay for in advance, would be guaranteed to produce the castings for at least 100,000 blocks.

"We'll give you a written quotation in a week or so for the cost of the die, and for casting sets in minimum runs," the engineer said.

At this point in time, I stopped in again to visit my old pal Bill Wild. He was as busy and as totally involved as ever, and seemed to be a little uptight from nervous strain. His record of success came at the cost of total involvement—high pressure on every project, worrying how to underbid his competitors in ship repair yet show a profit on every job.

"Bill, we're growing fast, and I need help in the business. Would you consider coming in with me for a decent salary and a bunch of company stock—be a part owner?" I said after visiting for a while.

"Well, you know what I've been working for all these years as well as I do. You remember from the start, I wanted to be in a position in top management, with a good salary, in a sound company, with retirement on down the road. I've got a family to support, two kids to finish college, a good salary—I'll be a vice president soon, and besides, they're about to move this ship repair operation to San Diego, where they are depending on me to be general manager. So that all means I've made it to my career goal, and it looks like you've just about made your career goal," Bill said. So, with handshakes and best wishes for good health and success, I left. This was the last get-together of the two Bills.

We received quotations for injection mold castings the next week. The price of the die was something over $22,000. We were absolutely sure we could justify a cash outlay of this amount for tooling. The new tooling would allow us substantially greater profits from the already popular hand line block. But to pay out the money, plus thousands more for advertising, a paint booth, parts inventory, and so on, would deplete operating capital below the danger point. The problem was how to come up with the money without depleting capital and/or selling a lot of company stock.

At lunch with Bob Miller, we kicked around the financial problem. During his career, he had experienced several similar problems. He suggested, and I agreed, that the Small Business Administration should be checked out for the possibility of a loan. So with the injection mold quotation in hand, I stopped by the busy Portland office of SBA. I was escorted to the office of a courteous interviewer, who listened and asked questions as I told my story. He then explained the SBA program. At that time, SBA made direct loans to businesspeople—there was no bank involved in their loans. The maximum loan to a qualified company was $25,000.

The first step in qualifying for a loan for a businessman was to show the SBA letters from two banks turning down our loan application.   Then there were several other forms to fill out along with our audited company financial statements, and CPA-prepared personal financial statements. The consequences of defaulting on a loan would mean all of the defaulter's assets would be available to SBA to sell to repay the loan. The SBA interest rate was 5.5 percent,versus 8 percent for a bank loan at that time.

After discussing the situation with Virgil the banker, and the two Bobs—McFarlane the CPA and Miller the foundry president—I decided to go after the loan. The first step was to apply for a loan of $25,000 at two banks. I felt pretty sure they would turn me down because of my lack of credit history with them. That was the easy part. The refusal letters were in hand, and the accountants were working on the financial statements required for the application.

At that time in the fall of 1963, it was necessary for me to travel to Washington, D.C., to meet with the Technical Standards Committee at the Rural Electrification Administration, located in the Department of Agriculture building. Ernie Moreland, standards engineer and Stan Vest, chief engineer, were both helpful. Ernie provided me with all the forms and procedures required and introduced me to other associates in the office. This was the first of many pleasant meetings with Ernie and Stan, often involving a luncheon meeting.

After winding things up at the REA, I hailed a cab and headed for Senator Wayne Morse's office. The senator had told me previously, during visits in Oregon, to stop in and see him if I visited Washington, D.C. I was in the city, and now I had axes to grind. Senator Morse was a member of the Small Business Committee and was influential. I wanted to consult with him regarding my upcoming SBA application.

Senator Morse greeted me cheerfully, introduced his staff, and took the time to hear all about my SBA application. He seemed to be as excited as I about the possibilities of marketing the hand line block. His reply to my question about who I should talk with in government about my application was: "Talk to no one. At the bottom of any correspondence with SBA in the future, just show a carbon copy to Senator Morse, Washington, D.C. My office will maintain a file on the application."

My letter to SBA Portland, forwarding all of the required loan application documents, as well as all correspondence that followed, always had "c/c Senator Wayne Morse" at the bottom. It was very doubtful the Senator ever mentioned anything to anyone at the Capitol about my loan application. The appearance of his name on my letters apparently was an incentive for those involved at the various levels of the bureaucracy to give it priority. Instead of the six to eight weeks I was told it would take to process the application, the note was forwarded to me for signature in less than three weeks.

Also nice was the stipulation in the note that the first monthly payment would be due six months after the date of the note. This would give us time for the new castings to become available and production to be under way. The note provided for $25,000, with interest at 5.5 percent, with installments, principal, and interest of $440 payable monthly for six years. Each installment was paid every month at least one week before it was due, per advice from banker friend Solso. The note was stamped "Paid in Full" on December 12, 1969, a few days less than six years after the note was signed.

This one transaction with Small Business Administration made it possible for our small company to exploit a niche in the market by going national quickly with a quality product, securing our place in the market before competitors could tool up to copy the block. The block served as a tremendous boost to our program. Our company could now mass-produce the hand line block in a fraction of the time, and at a fraction of the cost, with the injection molded parts. The very attractive and obviously high-quality design became sort of a status symbol for our company. Before long, it was being exported to many foreign countries. I have seen linemen using our hand line block from Taiwan to Saudi Arabia, and in many other countries.

When traveling around the U.S. and abroad, making business calls on electric utilities, I always carried a hand line block with me. Regardless which of our product lines were being discussed, I would place the hand line block on my customer's desk.

"You might be interested in looking at one of our products. It's the smallest item we manufacture, and the only one I can take along with me on my travels. It's representative of all our products in workmanship and quality," I would say.

Often the person across the desk was an electric utility executive, possibly a purchasing agent or a power distribution superintendent. They were all impressed, holding it for long periods of time, noticing how freely the sheave would spin on ball bearings, studying the construction, asking questions.

What puzzled everyone was the fact the two sides of the block were riveted together at the bottom, but the nuts securing the sheave axle were both recessed into the side castings.

"How in hell do you turn these nuts on?" many would say.

"To guarantee the nuts would never work off the axle and drop a load, we made the nuts captive. In the assembly, we place a nut in each side casting cavity, and then turn the nut and side castings together, as a unit, onto each end of the axle. The side castings are then turned until the bottoms of the side castings join. Then a roll pin is installed with end caps to complete the job," I said.

Before leaving the Small Business Administration, I must comment on the fine cooperation and helpful advice received from SBA during the six years we were paying installments on the note. Our file at SBA was assigned to Mr. Green. According to our loan agreement, it was necessary to visit with him regularly, to go over our year-end profit and loss statements. His background in accounting and business management and his sincere desire to help, soon showed him to be another valued consultant. Also, here was another pair of knowledgeable eyes to review all aspects of our operations, from outside the company looking in, with no axes to grind. His effort was to keep me on the straight and narrow and from failures others had experienced.

I really appreciated his input and told him so many times. Years later, the Small Business Administration named me Oregon's Small Businessman of the Year. I doubt Mr. Green or the loan had anything to do with the award, which was more to do with our rate of growth in the U.S. and export markets.

The hand line block was indeed a success, but more than that, it represented the reward of some twenty years of preparation and job experience, aimed at someday building my own company to manufacture products for the electric utility industry. We considered the improvements we had made to the hand line block would not be patentable, so we did not apply.

At about this time Dave Brewer, our attorney, resigned from the Board of Directors. Bob Miller had also resigned from the

Board, having retired from his company. Our friend Don McEwen, a trial lawyer and partner in one of Portland's oldest law firms, joined the Board as secretary.

15

Growing Pains: More Products Require More Space

During my visits with linemen and safety engineers in the utilities to check out hand line block design details, I was alerted several times about another tool needing development—larger, stronger, safer rigging blocks than those in use by the utilities. Almost all power company line trucks carried two sizes of rigging blocks. The six-inch diameter sheave size was rated at 5,000 pounds safe working load, and the eight-inch diameter sheave size at 8,000 pounds. Like the old hand line blocks, the heavy rigging blocks were designed for general use in industry. Some were of high quality, some definitely were not, and certainly none was designed for use by linemen.

Claude Haggard, safety engineer for California-Oregon Power Company, called one day.

"Hey Bill, your hand line blocks are fine, no problems, but now we are very interested in examining a rope block designed with safety features for linemens' use. Drop in to see me next time you are in town." Claude was known as "Mr. Safety" because of his lectures to the public on safe electrical practices.

The rigging block Claude referred to was used by linemen for hoisting heavy loads, hundreds or thousands of pounds. To hoist a transformer from street level to high up on power poles, for example, they would attach a rope block to the top of the power pole, then run a heavy manila rope through the block and down to ground level to the line truck, which had a power-operated capstan. By wrapping a few turns of rope around the capstan, and attaching the other end of the rope to the transformer, they could lift it safely to pole top, guided by the ground man and controlled by the man operating at the capstan. Some safety people in the utilities considered rope blocks a safety hazard, at least in the way the linemen used them, and many accidents were recorded owing to failure of rope blocks. Here was another product development possibility.

Redesign of the rope block for utility use was another job for Bob Miller and his light metals expertise. We decided to follow the general design of the popular Skookum steel rope block made in the area. We would use magnesium in place of steel in the side castings, use an aluminum sheave, redesign top fittings for safety, cast safe working load figures in raised letters on the side castings, and include a blank space for a test certificate number. The standard steel six-inch rigging block the linemen were using weighed twenty-five pounds. Our lightweight block weighed twelve and one-half pounds. We were sure the linemen who worked with them every day would appreciate the lighter weight.

I took one of the redesigned blocks with me on my next visit to Medford with Claude, the safety engineer. He was delighted with the appearance, weight and obvious safety features. Claude suggested we leave the block with a line crew to use and evaluate for the next thirty days until my next visit. This was the crew the utility used to try out new tools for evaluation before purchasing.

A month later I was with Claude again. I told him the sample block I left with the crew was the only one in existence, and we needed it back at the factory for pattern adjustments and various changes. He gave me the name of the crew foreman who had the block. A call to dispatching told me where the crew was working, not far from downtown Medford. I drove out and found them.

"Hi, Mac. I'm checking the block I left with you last month. Did the crew try it out? Were there any complaints?" I said to the line foreman.

"Hell no, they haven't used an old steel block all month. They liked it a lot."

Then I told him I had to take it back to the factory to tool up for production runs. Mac started asking the crew for the block, one at a time. No one knew where it was.

"Maybe we left it in the tall grass at that last job. Sorry about that," he said. I knew the guys were blowing smoke, and was delighted.

These were professional linemen who had been around for a long time. It was obvious they liked the block and did not want to give it up. They were not bashful. If they had any criticism, I would have heard all about it in their unvarnished language. Claude finally had to throw his weight around to recover the block for me, and next morning he told me the block would be their standard from then on.

This new model rigging block (Plate 7) was different from all other rigging blocks, and I thought it should have a trade name to distinguish it from ordinary blocks. The name "Blockmaster" seemed to fit the product, and we filed for and received copyright protection for our line of rope blocks. The copyright would prevent any other company from using the name Blockmaster in their advertising or product labeling. We considered the improvements we had made to the snatch blocks would not be patentable, so did not apply.

S hop space in Chip's warehouse was getting pretty crowded. We started looking seriously for a larger, inexpensive manufacturing space. Business was coming in fast with Joe Shelley and a new salesman doing their jobs. Block business particularly was booming.

We noticed an ad placed in the newspaper by the State of Oregon Highway Department. A building in inventory would be demolished in a year or so, owing to highway construction. The Marshall building had 5,000 square feet of space, and the rent was $200 per month. Availability was guaranteed for one year, and monthly thereafter. It had an office in front and a well-lighted shop/warehouse in the rear.

We signed the papers for a year or more if available. We all pitched in, working nights and weekends, moving out of Chip's warehouse, and moving offices out of the Schmitt building and into the Marshall building.

Working extra hours and with no outside help, we had the building in production in one week, which pointed out what a unique group of people we had at Western Power Products. We would not hire contractors to do work we could do ourselves, such as moving, carpentry, painting, electric wiring, or plumbing. We enjoyed the challenge, enjoyed doing something different, and certainly enjoyed working together. Also, we saved a lot of money, which we could use as operating capital.

We added more shop workers as orders for blocks, mast arms, brackets, and substations kept coming in as we expanded our product line, while at the same time selling the products of manufacturers we represented.

The next product development began with a conversation with Joe Shelley. Joe told me about a promising new product that had been developed by two of our power company friends. One was an electrical engineer in the distribution department, Joe Williams. The other was a division district manager, Perry Landsom.

As Joe told it, Williams and Landsom had worked up a machine called a tensioner, consisting of a series of rubber-lined, grooved wheels aligned so that an electric conductor (or "wire") could be directed through the machine. The machine was anchored to the rear end of a line truck.

Mounted on the line truck was a large reel of electric conductor. When the conductor was fed through the machine and up a series of power poles, the tensioner would prevent the conductor from sagging down to ground level between power pole supports as it was being pulled in. The tensioner was in fact an adjustable brake, holding back conductor as it was being installed.

It was necessary for the conductor to remain taut while being installed to allow traffic to move under it, to prevent damage to the conductor, reduce labor, and so on. Joe and Perry wanted to demonstrate the tensioner to us the following Saturday at the power company storage yard. They also wanted to discuss the possibility of our manufacturing and marketing it.

Shelley and I showed up first thing Saturday morning to find Joe and Perry busy setting up a tensioner, which was bolted to the rear of a line truck. They had strung some aluminum conductor from the reel on the truck through the tensioner, and attached the free end of the cable to another line truck about 100 feet away from the tensioner.

When given the word, the far truck moved on down the yard. Perry worked the controls on the tensioner, and sure enough, the conductor came up as tight as a violin string, with practically no visible sag in a 150-foot span. Joe and Perry stood there grinning while Shelley and I scratched our heads. The principle worked. The machine was crude, but it proved a point. Joe and Perry had a patent pending on the tensioner.

We broke for lunch and talked it all over. Joe and Perry wanted us to manufacture and market the tensioner, and pay them a royalty on each machine sold. Fair enough. We would take over, manufacture a few to determine our costs, do some market research, and between us arrive at a fair royalty. We shook hands on the deal, with no lawyers, just the four of us.

Normally, Joe and Perry would have engaged a good attorney to draft a contract between them and WPP, because of the tendency of some manufacturers to cheat inventors. However, we were all good friends. A handshake was our contract. No way would any of us back down on our word.

We built a couple of tensioners using the same materials and methods as the original, to establish base costs to use as a starting point. The upper and lower frames had been formed out of steel plate, bent in the shape of a "U." The very slight variations in dimensions from one frame to another, typical in formed steel sheets, made volume production of other components impossible, just as it was our experience with hand line block castings.

On a hunch, I called my friends at Kaiser Aluminum and asked if a channel, equivalent in dimensions to the steel channel on the tensioner, could be extruded in aluminum. They told me they could, but it was as large as they could go. The cost was about $200, which was less than the formed steel plate, but more important, every extruded channel would be of exactly the same dimensions. It was strong and lightweight, and it allowed us to make production runs of the components that mounted on the frames. Simply put, the aluminum extrusion process squeezes a mass of aluminum, under extremely high pressure, through an opening in a die plate. The opening is of the exact dimensions as the desired end product—a long bar formed in a "U" shape.

We made other changes to parts of the tensioner, such as redesigning the means of applying hydraulic pressure to the braking system, and the means of directing the conductor from a cable reel into the tensioner, for which I received a patent (see Plates 8 and 9). These improvements simplified the operation of the tensioner, and it worked perfectly.

Conductor tensioners had been in use for dozens of years working as a brake while pulling in electrical conductor for power lines. The tensioners were massive pieces of equipment mounted on a large lowboy trailer, along with reels of electrical conductor, the trailer connected to a line truck. It was necessary to park the trailer so that the tensioner was lined up in the direction the conductor was to be strung, usually blocking traffic in the process. The old tensioner models also required several men to handle the process. The cost of the new tensioner was far less than the older models, and it was light enough to be lifted in place by two men.

One of the good points of the tensioner development was the fact that Joe and Perry recognized a problem, considered solutions and then did something about it. We introduced the tensioner and sold many of them all over the U.S. and in foreign countries. The electric power line contractors particularly liked the new tensioner, because it took fewer men to operate and was faster and less expensive. We even equipped the Taiwan Power Company, Republic of China, with all their tensioners. Because of our patents, we could afford to use high-quality parts and make a good profit, knowing that no competitor could price us out of the market.

We had a fine, friendly relationship with Joe and Perry, which was unusual between inventors and a patent licensee, because of disputes over royalty payments. However, from the beginning we issued them monthly statements, listing each unit sold by serial number, customer, and sale price. We always attached a check covering the total royalties. There never was a problem addressed by either side.

After a couple of years, as sales continued to increase, Joe and Perry suggested we talk about Western Power Products purchasing their patent. The tensioner royalty payments were the only source of income for their company, L&W, and the tax laws required they turn over the lion's share of their royalties to Uncle Sam. So together we worked out a formula for placing a value on their patent and gave them a check for all future patent rights.

In September 1963 we hired Jim Coon as a salesman. Jim had worked as a salesman for Maydwell & Hartzell in southern Oregon for a few years. Prior to that he had worked for Portland General Electric Company as a lineman and a line foreman. A hard-working fellow, he would be of great value to the company in future years, particularly in communicating details of our product developments to electric utilities.

The Marshall building had worked out well. We were taking on more and more work every month, and it had to pass through the shop, so we were very mindful of the fact that it would be necessary for the company to be moving again soon. Our agreement with the State of Oregon was good only to July 1, 1964, and then it was month to month. The closer we approached July, the harder we looked for something suitable within the city core area of Portland. The core area was important because the common carrier freight trucks would pick up and deliver freight at no extra charge within their city core zone. In our business, freight costs ran up fast.

It was in October of 1964 that I noticed a "For Lease" sign on a commercial building in our neighborhood. The building was on a corner at an intersection of two busy through streets and extended through one city block. I called the number on the sign and made an appointment to look over the building.

The building was in very good condition. The office spaces facing the street were roomy and adequate, the warehouse well lighted and in good shape. The building had been built and used for years as a regional distribution point by a national manufacturer of wire rope. The wire rope was shipped in large reels made of wood or steel, which was probably why the warehouse floor was made of thick oak planks. The center aisle showed some wear, but the oak was in excellent condition everywhere else.

After reviewing all of the building, inside and out, we discussed the fact that the wood floor would not work for our company, because of the welding, burning and other machine shop operations. The only way we could consider a lease would be to remove the wood and lay in concrete. Mr. Goodman said he would have no objection.

"Well sir, then there is a possibility of our interest in the building. Hopefully, you will take this costly floor repair into consideration when arriving at a base figure," I said.

The building had been vacant for some time, probably due to the fire hazard of its wooden floor. He indicated he was prepared to offer a very reasonable five-year lease. We haggled a bit about lease cost, and arrived at a monthly rental rate of $405. The building was 10,000 square feet, so considering the location and condition, the rent was a real bargain.

I told him I needed to get my board together to discuss the lease. "I'll get back to you with our decision within a week," I said.

B ack at the office the next morning, thinking about the discussion with Mr. Goodman and his obvious desire to get rid of his building, I thought it worthwhile to try another angle. I called him and said, "I have been on the phone with two of our directors. They are interested to know what would be your best price for sale of the building, whether you would offer us a five-year lease agreement including an option for our purchase of the building for the amount you quote, at any time during the five-year lease." He said he would call me back.

The reason for my bringing up the purchase angle was that it had always been my belief that lease payments on our company buildings were lost forever, of no future value to us. Mortgage payments, on the other hand, built equity in the building. Property values in good locations increased through the years. The building, increasing in value, then would become an asset base for the company.

While the Goodman negotiations were going on, we were sweating out the deal with the State Highway Department. Every time the mail came in, we were expecting a notice to vacate within thirty days. However, Mr. Goodman came back with his deal. He offered a five-year lease at the price we previously agreed on, but he also offered to include an option for us to purchase the building at any time during the lease period for $50,000. After approval by our attorney and accountant, we accepted the deal, and signed the papers with the lease to start December 15, 1964.

We laid out the shop area in one-third of the warehouse space. Then I called in a wood remanufacturing company to give us a quotation for removal of the oak flooring in the shop area and aisle, and to haul it away to their plant. They were delighted to see all of the solid oak and gave us a good price offer. They cleared it all out in just a few days. Then we took bids from three contractors to fill and lay a concrete floor. We came out several hundred dollars ahead of the game. What had seemed to be a liability to others who had considered purchase of the property turned out instead to be an asset. There was another benefit in changing the floor. We were able to do the subfloor wiring and piping before the concrete was laid, saving us the trouble of trenching the floor later.

For the time being, we had plenty of office, shop, and warehouse space. Once again, John, Jim, Herb, Joe, and I made the move. We installed lighting, benches, machinery, and other equipment. Next we had a Western Power Products sign painted across the front of the building.

By this time our company was pretty well established as manufacturers' representatives for Allis-Chalmers, Schmitt Steel, and Pacific Light Metals Foundry. We were also established as manufacturers of hand line and rope blocks, power line construction tools and packaged substations. We had one more item to develop in line construction tools—a wheel chock for line trucks.

What got this project under way was a request by Fons Hughes, safety engineer for Pacific Power & Light Company. It seems another local utility had a line truck parked on a hilly street in Oregon City one morning while the crew was having coffee in a nearby restaurant. They left the engine running, which was normal, so they could hear radio calls. The electric brakes on the line truck accidentally let go, and the line truck went bouncing down the hill, hitting parked cars, store fronts, and power poles, finally coming to rest against a building, all smashed up. The accident caused Fons to review their vehicle safety practices and procedures. The wheel chocks carried on their trucks were inadequate.

"Hey, Bill, see what you can come up with in a chock that will fit our trucks, and that the crews will use," Fons said.

It was a project for Bob Miller. I sketched out a shape of a chock, based on the diameter of a truck wheel, and asked Bob to design it to withstand the loaded weight of a line truck, around 25,000 pounds.

We decided on heat-treated aluminum as a material for the chock. It was to be lightweight, so that truck drivers would be more inclined to use it than if we used heavy steel.

The chock Bob produced looked rugged and functional and weighed only six pounds (see Plate 10). I took it to a power company garage and asked my friend Claude if he could have a loaded line truck drive up on top of the chock as a strength test. The chock performed well, restraining the truck, even on the smooth concrete floor of the garage. Next, we had to design a catalog sheet to distribute to the electric utilities.

While the wheel chock development was going on, the local newspaper carried a story about a runaway garbage truck, along with a picture of the truck resting comfortably across the top of an automobile. The report said the garbage truck drove up a steep driveway incline to pick up the garbage at an apartment building. While the driver was out of the truck, again the electric brakes failed.

The truck took off backwards, down the steep driveway and across the street, bounced up over a curb, and smashed through a steel pipe railing fence, landing on top of a fairly new car parked at a lower level. No one was in the car, fortunately.

The picture on the front page of the newspaper was quite graphic—better than a thousand words. I called the paper and asked to talk to the photographer. I told him we would like to purchase the film of the garbage truck caper. He sold it to us for $10. It was the perfect picture for the catalog sheet. We sold thousands of the wheel chocks. The picture told a great story about Murphy's law and its economic consequences.

From time to time we produced other line construction tools, including rope capstans and large transmission line stringing sheaves in magnesium. The Los Angeles Department of Water and Power used our stringing sheaves to install the transmission line across the Harbor Freeway. After a couple of years, though, we decided to get out of the stringing sheave business. Most sales were made to power line contractors, and most of them were slow about paying their bills, unlike electric utilities, which paid promptly.

Of course, there were some nice line contractors, such as one who called me one day from Illinois, and praised our tensioner. "I've just finished pulling a million feet of conductor through my LW-100 tensioner, and I want to buy another. Tell me the price, so I can send my check with the order," he said.

Manufacturers used job shops for a number of different reasons. In our shops, we limited our installed machinery to equipment we would have regular and frequent use for, so components we chose not to fabricate, we farmed out. It was however, most important for us to have control of the final assembly, test, inspection, packaging and shipment of all of our products.

As the company moved along into the fifth, sixth and seventh years, volume was building steadily, and earnings were increasing every year. We never had an annual operating loss. However, as sales activities increased, we needed more people to service the accounts. We had a shop crew to manage, product development activity, and factory rep activity, all of which required planning, supervision, and management. Future profitable growth would require adding more management staff to the company. Individuals who qualified with management talents frequently wanted "a piece of the action." Western Power Products was a corporation, so management people would want the right to purchase stock.

The sale of corporate stock required a great deal of thought by me, since I was the majority stockholder. We were organized as a closely held corporation. Our shares of stock were not available for sale to the general public, and we were authorized to issue stock to a limited number of shareholders. It was my intention to retain in my personal file, aside from company treasury stock, something over 50 percent of the number of shares we issued, so that I could maintain voting control of the company.

We would not sell stock to raise capital. Stock would be made available to a limited number of individuals who we considered to be important to the management or success of the company. The dollar value of a share of stock was determined by the last reported net worth (in dollars) of the company divided by the number of outstanding shares sold to shareholders.

The only string we tied to a sale of our stock was that the purchaser would need to agree that if he ever wished to sell the stock, the stock must first be offered to our company to buy back within a ninety-day period. The buy-back price for the stock would be determined by the same formula as used when it was purchased.

There were good points and bad points about selling corporate stock to key employees. The good points included the tendency of most people owning shares to have a continuing interest in helping the company prosper, because, of course, as the company prospered and the net worth increased, the value of all outstanding shares increased. This is what happened at Maydwell & Hartzell, when Pop was unable to acquire any shares to sell to me. With the stock increasing in value every year, no one wanted to sell.

However, the bad points about selling stock to key employees could apply to any young, fast-growing, profitable company, such as WPP, where an employee's instinct of greed tended to overpower the other human traits of character and fair play. Once a share of stock was sold out of treasury stock to any employee, there was no way to force the employee to sell it back to the company. If a key employee stockholder decided to leave the company and set up his own company in direct competition with his former employer, he would continue to have access to his former employer's financial reports, profit and loss statements, and the like, as long as he owned a share of stock.

This devious behavior happened at WPP more than once. Key employee stockholders resigned after carefully collecting engineering data, customer lists, marketing information, pricing data, and copies of our records for their future use. In one case, we introduced the individual to the packaged substation business, and ultimately placed him in charge, and paid him a fair salary plus bonuses and stock. He suddenly resigned, took his assistant with him, and set up as a competitor.

In another case, we placed an individual in charge of certain manufacturers' rep sales. One such product had great promise of future sales. We spent thousands of dollars introducing the product, and in marketing efforts in the Northwest. Here again, we paid the individual well, with annual bonus and company stock, and had a congenial family relationship. We arranged for him to make visits to the factory we were representing for latest product information. However, he used the factory visits to lobby the manufacturer to cancel WPP and take him as their rep. The change was a complete surprise to WPP.

On the other side of the coin, the great majority who owned stock were fine, loyal people who made major contributions to the rapid growth of the company, and the professionals who were stockholders guided us in the legal, accounting and financial areas through the years.

There were also, we might add, many staff employees who owned no stock and were hard-working, dedicated people. Many stayed with the company through the years and made great contributions to our success. We never refused to sell stock to any employee who asked for it, but neither did we try to sell them stock.

The bad apples were mentioned only to point out that the success of any new and growing company depends to a great degree on its employees—particularly the key and supervisory employees—and as the company grew, it becomes necessary to delegate more and more responsibilities to more and more employees. Greed sometimes changes the trusted employee to an imposter. Although his tactics were probably legal, there was no basis for calling the imposter's actions morally correct. The people who used this tactic to launch their independent careers seldom profited for very long.

We certainly had no problem with employees moving on. We would give letters of recommendation when appropriate, and wish the employee the best of luck.

I firmly believe that an employee planning to leave his employer to start a similar company should do the honorable thing: give weeks or months of notice (depending on his status in the company) in writing. His employer should be assured the employee will not directly compete in the same market as his employer, or reveal any of his employer's sensitive trade secrets.

16

Develop and Patent the Fiberglass Equipment Enclosure

In the mid-1960s the electric utilities in the Pacific Northwest started thinking seriously about eliminating conventional overhead pole line construction standards in certain selected areas, such as new residential and commercial developments. This new look would involve installing all electrical conductors underground wherever possible.

Accordingly, the developer of a new coastal destination resort at Gleneden Beach in Oregon's Lincoln County required electric and telephone conductors to be installed underground. The name of this resort was Salishan, and it was to be the largest resort of its kind on the Pacific Coast. The layout included a central lodge, dozens of private homesites, and a beautiful golf course, all with sweeping ocean views. No power poles were to be allowed.

Although it had been common practice for years to serve certain customers underground from an adjacent power pole, Salishan would be a different experience. Pacific Power & Light Company, the utility serving the project, had no precedent or standards at that time to provide service underground to such a large project.

Tim O'Keefe was PP&L's standards engineer. Tim spear-
headed the program to develop new practices and procedures for
the Salishan electrical distribution system. I became involved in
the development of a series of steel cabinets of various sizes, to
enclose fuses, transformers and switches. The cabinets were to be
installed at ground level, fastened to concrete pads, and arranged
for connection to electrical cables coming up from underground
and inside the cabinets. The cabinets had to be rugged in design.
The door, with special padlocks, would be accessible to power
company personnel only. Particular attention was paid to the paint
specifications, because the cabinets would be installed in full view
of the public and would be subject to corrosion from the coastal
salt air.

We received a purchase order for twenty cabinets of various
sizes to get manufacturing started, along with PP&L drawings and
specifications. We farmed out the work for the steel cabinets and
did the mounting of interior equipment, installed vents, and sprayed
on the base coats and finish coats of the specified coatings. The
cabinets were then carefully wrapped, crated and shipped to Pacific
Power & Light.

As the first shipment of cabinets were being installed, we
received orders for more of the same, but then some bad news.
Some of the top brass at PP&L had visited Salishan with the devel-
opers, and noticed streaks of rust on the cabinets after only six
months on the project. A hurried trip to Salishan provided us with
the answer.

During transportation, delivery and installation, the paint had
been scraped off around some of the edges, perhaps from the use of
wire rope slings. Management decided steel was out as cabinet
material but did not know what else to use.

We considered cabinets of the same design but in an
aluminum alloy that would not rust. The engineers nixed the bare
aluminum. We could find no protective coating for aluminum that
would withstand the corrosive sea air, much less the handling of
installation crews. Aluminum was definitely out.

Fiberglass was a possibility. I knew next to nothing about the
material, but I did know it could not rust, being composed of

organic resins, and the surfaces could be prepared to look as nice as painted surfaces. The engineers agreed to look into it.

What was needed next was a consultant knowledgeable with the fiberglass industry. I thought the best way to find one would be to call some suppliers of fiberglass material and ask who among the manufacturers they serviced was the most knowledgeable person in Oregon in the development of specialized fiberglass products. Most of the suppliers I talked with recommended Carl Brennan of Highway Products Company in Canby, Oregon. Carl's plant produced a very popular model of fiberglass boat.

Carl proved to be just the right person to work on our problem. We reviewed the steel cabinet drawings and discussed impact resistance of fiberglass and so forth.

"The major change in design from metal to fiberglass would be the need to split the cabinet vertically in halves, making three individual parts—a front section with door opening, a rear section and a door," he said.

To complete the enclosure, the two halves would fit together, secured by bolts and resin cement. The door would be a lift-off type, properly secured. An internal flange around the bottom would provide strength and a means of bolting the enclosure to the concrete pad.

We chose a dark shade of green for a finished color and asked Carl to make an inexpensive mold to produce one part for customer approval. We also required price estimates, specification sheets, and a few sample fiberglass panels for tests by the customer.

The first sample part was ready in about two weeks. The enclosure looked pretty good to me. We took it to our shop to install padlock hasps and vent screens, then delivered it to PP&L. We designated the part a fiberglass equipment enclosure. The sample was approved. As far as we knew, it was the first of its kind ever produced. We were told to proceed with models of three other sizes needed for the Salishan project.

Although the enclosures were quite angular in appearance, similar to metal enclosures, the corners were well rounded, and the roof was raised slightly from the sides up to the seam, so it looked better than the steel models. Carl was most cooperative with us during the development period.

We had the feeling, after completion and acceptance of the sample part, that this new product could well be the start of another major product development, far more important than all our other new products to date. Carl agreed to make production molds for the other enclosure sizes we might need, and to fit production of enclosures in with his production of boats, he would start a night shift if necessary.

We wasted no time in telling our other customers about our fiberglass enclosures, resulting in good sales volume the first year. Even though we were experiencing good acceptance and sales and could see tremendous new application possibilities coming up, we were not at all satisfied with the two-part design. Very often the parts required grinding to fit properly, or were rejected because of slight color differences or other flaws. These problems could be eliminated if we could find a way to mold the enclosure in one piece.

The reason the enclosure could not be molded in one piece was that the radius of the doorframe extended inside the enclosure to make it tamper proof. Also, a flange extended inward around the bottom surfaces to provide for mounting to a concrete pad. If the fiberglass were sprayed on the inside surfaces of a one-piece mold, the part would be locked in place, with no way to remove it. We deliberated among ourselves for a single-part solution and also queried suppliers of resin and fiberglass. They offered no suggestions.

Enclosure sales were increasing every month. There was absolutely nothing like them on the market anywhere in the U.S. Carl started complaining that he had reached capacity and suggested we find another source or set up our own fiberglass shop. We did find another shop to make parts from our molds, giving Carl some relief. The new fiberglass shop started producing enclosure parts, but the quality of their parts was very poor.

Our production problems were brought into sharp focus one evening in October 1968. After the night shift employees in Carl's plant had left for the day, the plant caught fire and burned to the ground. The late shift had failed to remove fiberglass waste material from the plant, and it was ignited by spontaneous combustion. Fortunately, our molds were stored outside the building. Carl had told me previously he had to self-insure his building, and that insurance companies expected all fiberglass spray-up plants to burn down eventually. After the fire he decided not to rebuild.

All of this resulted in a genuine crisis right when our enclosure business was moving along just fine. It was time now to find another building, and also time for us to find out what there was to know about the business of chopper gun lay-up of fiberglass parts. At this point in time, no one in the company had any knowledge of fiberglass production.

After checking with city hall, I found it to be illegal to manufacture fiberglass within the Portland city limits because of the fire hazard. Therefore, we located a building outside the city limits that had many limitations, but it was available for a five-year lease, with no restrictions on producing fiberglass. We recruited Carl's crew, now out of a job. With their help we purchased large air compressors, exhaust fans, chopper guns, and various other equipment. Our WPP crew went all out, working nights and weekends to prepare the shop for fiberglass. As soon as the heavy equipment arrived, the shop was ready to make our first parts, and I was ready to watch, ask questions, listen, and learn.

We had one more year to go on our five-year lease with Mr. Goodman for our office/shop building. We could purchase the building at any time during the five-year lease, but we were outgrowing the building, so we decided to try to sell it for a profit, pay off Mr. Goodman, and invest any profit in a larger building.

The building lease with option to purchase for a stated amount during the lease period provided an opportunity to move from lease/rental to building owner—to establish a new asset base for the company.

We placed an ad in the newspaper, and within a few days sold it for seventy-five thousand dollars. However, before we could complete the sale, we had to pay off Mr. Goodman's $50,000, so we would have clear title. The offer of seventy-five thousand dollars was verbal, so I asked the company to present their offer in writing, confirming terms as cash.

I had previously looked at a building one-half mile from downtown Portland. It was located on two acres and the building covered 22,000 square feet. The owner, Mr. Brice, was a local bank president. The listed price was $200,000, with $50,000 required as a down payment. The building suited our needs just fine, but how would we come up with $50,000 without dangerously depleting our working capital? We talked it over at a board meeting and decided to try to find a way to purchase the property.

I made an appointment with Mr. Brice and explained our reasons for wanting to buy his building, if we could make the down payment, and if his bank would carry the mortgage for the remainder. After examining our financial statements, he finally stood up, shook hands and said: "You've got a deal."

"That's fine, it's okay for the building, but I have another request," I said.

I explained my deal with Mr. Goodman and said I needed a $50,000 bridge loan to pay him off to secure the building title for transfer to the purchaser, and then I could collect the purchaser's offer of $75,000. I would use the $25,000 profit on the building sale plus $25,000 of our own funds for the down payment on his building.

"No problem. This is a win-win deal," he said. I did agree to change our banking over to his bank.

The building transaction was followed by a most important personal transaction. On the third day of September 1969, Joan Sanguras and I were married. Joan's son by a previous marriage, Larry Sanguras, having completed college and military service, would join the company and advance through the years to Vice President/Marketing and Production Control.

My daughters by a previous marriage, Mary Kepler and Betty Bright, would work to finish their education with master's degrees. Betty would move to the Midwest and marry Jay White. Mary Kepler would later become Mary Olson, and join the company as Cost Accountant. Joan assumed many tasks, including various duties on the Board of Directors, as well as assisting me wherever needed.

Through the first few years, we were in a learning mode in our fiberglass operations. Carl's former employees were a great help to us in getting the Clackamas plant going, and we produced many enclosures, transferring them to our Moody plant for finishing, installation of equipment, packaging, and shipment. Carl's men knew what to do about lay-up procedures, but not much beyond the process. The same was true of the people who made the molds.

The salesmen who sold us resin and fiberglass strand gave us lots of serious advice, but it was always slanted to benefit their particular supply business. As a result, we learned mostly by trial and error. We finally located a person who knew the answers about fiberglass mold design and construction, Brand Burrows. Brand had studied in the mold design area for years. Working with him, we developed the ultimate in fiberglass equipment enclosure design.

As noted earlier, it was our objective to find a way to make enclosures in one piece rather than in two halves. We had on file drawings we had made showing various models of sleek, ribbed one-piece enclosures. We felt the single-piece mold would work if we could somehow mount a removable mold the shape of a picture frame into the door opening of the enclosure mold, for removal after the spray-up and cure cycle, and before removing the enclosure. We discussed the idea with Brand, and he said it should work.

Seeing Brand work on this first mold project, we realized he was a remarkable craftsman. His objective was to make a fiberglass enclosure with doors on opposite sides, and measuring 50 inches wide, 46 inches deep, and 60 inches high, with sloping sides and vertical ribs.

The plug and mold enclosure process went well. The enclosure was removed from the mold after a twelve-hour cure and the doors installed. The result was outstanding (see Plate 11). We now had the key to producing very attractive, functional enclosures in one piece in practically unlimited shapes and sizes—thanks to the skills, from design drawing to finished product, of Brand

Burrows. It was now obvious this new design of equipment enclosure would be very marketable. It would completely fill the need for an enclosure to protect high voltage equipment mounted at ground level from access by unauthorized people.

Now it was time to talk to a patent attorney. My attorney, Don McEwen, suggested I contact the firm of Farley and Eckleman in Portland. As it worked out, Gene Eckleman was the person I talked with. We looked at photos and detailed drawings of our new enclosure. Gene asked lots of questions. He could see no chance of claiming patent rights for the enclosure as something unique. Already on the market were our two-piece enclosures, and lots of steel enclosures.

Gene suggested we try for a design patent, since the design was unique. The first step would be to have Gene's patent draftsman make up drawings as required by the U.S. Patent Office. My job was to assemble a full range of data for Gene, and to list every feature we considered unique. Our list of features included the requirement that the enclosure sides were to slope at an angle from the vertical of three degrees or more.

Gene advised us to immediately begin marking all advertising, cataloging, and labels "Patent Pending," as soon as we had filed the patent request. Since it took a year or more for the patent office to process a patent, the Patent Pending label would allow us to start shipping the new enclosures shortly after filing, with complete safety. The Patent Office would not disclose our claims until after the patent had been approved. We were now free to finish cataloging the new designs, and to make the important news release.

The application was approved by the Patent Office, along with our several claims, including the key claim of three degrees or more sloping sides. The patent was issued to me and proved to be just about as restrictive as any patent could be. Anyone who might try to copy our design in fiberglass, and to get around our patent by sloping the sides less than the "three degrees or more" claim, would find it impossible to remove the enclosure from the mold. We were aware of this physical design limitation when first working on the single-part concept. Through the years several individuals copied our design, but as soon as we were aware of it, a letter from our patent attorney always put an end to their infringement.

We all felt we had a real winner in the new model, but the only way to prove it was to make a market survey, so that electric utilities could have a hands-on introduction to our new equipment enclosure. We hired a new salesman, Dave Skeans, to make this survey. Dave was an ex-lineman, young and good-looking, who could talk "lineman" language. It was not difficult for Dave to make the choice between power line construction work and sales.

We had our shop make a lightweight, single-axle platform trailer, suitable for towing behind an automobile. We mounted our new enclosure on the trailer, along with a tension brake and other WPP products.

We told Dave we wanted him to make this important survey to find the answer to our major problem—what are the customers' reactions to these new products? The survey included making out a call report for every utility along the way, to record their reaction and comments. He was to travel south to Los Angeles and east to Florida, returning through the central part of the country. He could fly home to visit family every two weeks.

His survey made many valuable contacts for our company. His final report convinced us we were ready to go after the national market for all of our product line.

During 1971 we settled down in our new Moody building and were adding employees as order input increased every month. At this time we received a letter from the National Labor Relations Board (NLRB), advising us that our shop employees had voted to have the AFL/CIO union represent them in negotiations for wages and working conditions. This labor business came to us out of the blue. We had no idea our employees were dissatisfied or were talking to a union. Nearly every day I made it a point to walk through the shop, visiting the foremen and the people working at their jobs. Everything was congenial. Our wage scale and working conditions were comparable with union shops in the area. We purposely kept abreast of union shop pay scales, so that we could train and keep good employees.

Obviously it was much better for me to be able to contact my employees directly than to be forced by law to go through a third party, which was required in a union-controlled work force.

After the shock of the NLRB letter wore off a bit, I decided to consult with the very best labor attorney we could find to see us through the negotiations. Our local newspaper had been in labor negotiations which went on for months. Their attorney, Mr. Lubersky, received a lot of publicity and was very successful. I made an appointment to see him, and he agreed to take our case, at the same time advising me what steps to take in the initial contacts.

I was told much later by my employees that the union organizer made it a point to meet our shop employees a few at a time, sometimes over a beer after work, to talk union with them. He would see to it, if they voted for the union, that the company would pay them double what they were earning. After learning of the union promise, I complained about it to one of the attorneys. It was this promise of impossibly high wages that convinced the employees to vote union.

I was told that union organizers could tell prospective union converts just about anything they wished regarding promised wages. It was obvious, they told me, that the organizer had no power to pay the workers any kind of wages, so he could not be held accountable.

However, if I made such a promise, we could be held accountable because I did have the power to increase the wage level. This tactic on the part of the union organizer, conning vulnerable shop employees who knew nothing about NLRB laws or company financial operating ratios, did nothing to improve my negative image of big unions.

A few days after the Lubersky visit, we received a call from an attorney, Ken Jernstedt, advising that Lubersky had to leave town, and he was assigned to our case. Ken came to our office that day for our first meeting. He wanted to know everything about the company, the industry, and the product line. Ken took over from then on, writing the letters, arranging the meetings with the union people, and doing the actual negotiating. We had many meetings during July and through October.

The union wanted contracts to run from June to June, and over a two-year period. The company wanted November to November over a three-year period. Summer months were our busiest months. We did not want employees embroiled in union matters during our busiest season. The federal mediator became involved. It was settled with a November to November, over a three-year period. Another reason for our insisting on November to November—a strike could be called in June for frivolous reasons, during good vacation weather, whereas a November strike meant picket lines in cold weather.

The following two and one-half years moved along with practically no labor problems. However, beginning in January of the third year, we began hearing rumbles of discontent, and possibilities of a strike. When negotiations began in the fall of 1974, the letter from the union presented a list of demands. Our attorney filed their letter and demands, and prepared the company offer which would be the basis of the negotiations.

I chose not to attend labor/management meetings. I set the various limits beforehand, but left it up to Ken to do the negotiating.

After several meetings, the one sticking demand of labor was a contract retroactive to last June, then to run from June to June. Our answer was no.

"We get it or we walk," the union negotiator said.

"Looks like you're going to walk," Ken said.

The strike started the first week in December, involving only shop employees. The shop guys dutifully marched up and down the shop driveway, across the street from the office. The weather turned cold with snow and wind. The office people and shop supervisor continued assembly and shipment at a reduced scale. The office employees took coffee and doughnuts out to the strikers. The week before Christmas, the union advised that the strike was over. The contract would be based on our last offer. This was our first and only strike, and the beginning of much better relations between union reps and management.

Once in place, future contract negotiations went along quite smoothly, with Ken Jernstedt showing his leadership skills to all involved. The union, with their elected shop steward, did provide a measure of shop employee discipline, which is necessary in any type of group effort. I resumed personal contact with our shop employees as time moved along, and also introduced various forms of incentive pay for repetitive jobs, normally a union no-no. Among my impressions of our union experience was there would be a lot fewer strikes if all union contracts ran from November to November.

17

Sales Take Off in Domestic and Export Markets

Once we were settled in the Moody building, the first order of business was to review and organize our national sales program. Thanks to the years spent as a manufacturer's rep and sales engineer, I was quite familiar with the entire sales picture from purchasing agent to sales engineer to manufacturer's agent to manufacturer. Now I had to select the right agents.

The first I chose was easy: my old friend Petey Pederson, who had joined with another old friend to form Dwyer-Pederson Agency in Kentucky. A phone call was all that was needed.

After a review of territorial coverage of existing electric utility reps in the U.S., it appeared we would need about twenty reps for national coverage.

My method of locating good reps was to choose the largest electric utility within a recognized sales territory. A visit to the utility and an appointment to see the senior buyer would give me a chance to outline our product line, while he studied my sample hand line block. Then I would tell the buyer I was interested in locating a manufacturer's rep in the area to handle our product line, and ask him to suggest a few.

This question invariably produced two or three company names, along with a discussion of what made a good rep. Most purchasing department people tried to avoid showing any preference for one salesman over another. This would not be ethical, so usually it was a good bet that their third choice, or possibly the second choice, would be their real first choice. I could figure out who was number one after interviewing the reps.

There were many things we looked for in interviewing a prospective rep, but one good sign was that a rep needed one more good line to round out his other product lines. We would want no conflict with other lines he represented. We would want to know exactly what was his territory—the area he regularly covered, and his call frequency. Most important, was I comfortable in communicating with him?

We would estimate his annual sales volume to be earned selling our product line, first and second year, and advise him of the necessity of spending a week at our factory before starting to represent us. One of our factory people would make some initial calls with the new rep to answer customer queries.

The manufacturer's rep (also called a factory sales rep) was a rare type of entrepreneur. He was, without a doubt, a vital part of a manufacturer's marketing effort, both for product acceptance in the market and for continuity of sales. The good ones were hard to find and required very special consideration. There were, of course, many not-so-good reps who wanted to add as many lines as possible just to collect commissions while doing minimal work.

Finding a good rep in a foreign country was somewhat more difficult because of language and custom differences, but there were some very good ones. I felt a person needed several years working as a sales engineer, gaining experience such as I had with Maydwell & Hartzell, to become a good manufacturer's rep. This sales background was as important in foreign reps as in the United States. One good example was Jasper Ting, the best we ever dealt with. Jasper had headquarters in Taipei, Taiwan, and also in San Francisco. He set up his own manufacturer's rep company in Taiwan, after spending years as an employee of Minnesota Mining and Manufacturing (3M), selling their product line in Taiwan. As a result, he knew all about American ways of doing business, and as a sales engineer he was acquainted with all businesses throughout Taiwan, including Taiwan Power Company.

The Taiwan agent we had prior to Jasper was at the opposite end of the scale. A likable, energetic electrical engineer, he took over after we were already shipping switchgear enclosures to Taiwan Power.

After two years or so working with him, we heard from trade sources that he was in jail in Taipei. Apparently he had misrepresented the specifications of a certain foreign manufacturer to his customer. After that a mutual friend introduced us to Jasper Ting, who took over as our agent.

Some months later, Jasper advised us that Taiwan Power was complaining about the condition of some of our Powerglass enclosures installed in the Northwest coastal area of Taiwan. We promptly arranged a visit to Taiwan to check out the complaint. Jasper met my wife Joan and me and drove us out to the district headquarters, where we were joined by the district manager and a line crew. As we drove out to the area, we could see a cluster of enclosures in the distance. A few blocks away, Joan remarked that the enclosures were not the right color. She should know: she chose our standard color, willow green.

The closer we approached, the more obvious it was that these were very poor copies of our enclosures. Apparently, our former agent had had a mold made from one of our enclosures, then had a local shop produce several units which he represented as our products, charging Taiwan Power our prices. He made a bundle on this one sale, but it ended his sales career. The cobbled-up switchgear inside the enclosures also was a hazard to linemen and the public.

At Taiwan Power, our contacts were great about the entire incident, and the company continued as a loyal customer for many of our products. Jasper performed an outstanding job for our company, not only in handling our contacts with Taiwan Power but also in locating and monitoring sources to produce some of the components we used in our manufacturing.

As our sales volume increased in the product lines that had a potential of causing accidental injury to linemen and the public, we were reminded frequently by our insurance agent, Tom Galt, about our expanding exposure to product liability. Our products were in daily use across the country by linemen in their dangerous construction and repair activities. Moreover, our Powerglass enclosures, now installed in every state, were sitting ducks for everything from malicious mischief to vehicle accidents.

At least once a year, Tom needed to negotiate new rates for us with the insurance companies he dealt with. Our exposure to product liability was well known, so every year, it seemed, a new coverage would develop. Tom was a fighter on our behalf and succeeded in maintaining reasonable insurance rates through the years. He was able to maintain our good rates, he used to say, because we were extremely particular about the design, inspection, and testing of all of our products. Tom was proud of the fact (as we were) that through the years, we did not have a single product liability loss.

We also faced high fire insurance rates for our fiberglass operations. Tom would go through hours of work every year with his insurance companies because of our two fiberglass plants. He assured everyone that we were well aware of fire risks. Our personnel were trained to take fire prevention measures every day. A list of safety precautions was posted in each plant, and we required complete compliance.

We did have a small fire in one of our plants. The only damage was to the lay-up room, where fiberglass was sprayed onto molds. The cost was one day's production plus a chopper gun and a catalyst tank. No molds were lost. The fire station was only one block away, so the firemen saved the day. We located the employee who first saw the fire.

"Did you think to use the fire extinguisher mounted there on the wall?" I asked.

"Nope, I just ran like hell yelling fire," he said. A brave office staff member called the fire department. We never did put in a claim for fire insurance. Tom would have had a fit.

To make doubly sure this accident would never happen again, we moved the catalyst tank, the cause of the fire, out of the building. This was the one and only experience with fire in our plants.

In marketing our fiberglass enclosures, we recognized our number one national competitor as the McGraw-Edison Company, who marketed an enclosure made of sheets of steel bolted together. To save money, the power company customer could purchase the enclosure in pieces to assemble in the utility shop. The shop would not only assemble the enclosure but would also mount inside whatever electrical switchgear the job called for. Certain switchgear could be ordered from McGraw-Edison, but other equipment had to be ordered from General Electric or other manufacturers. All this was a bother and an overhead cost to the utility.

We had a good solution to this problem: let Western Power Products furnish not only our superior enclosures, but also all the switchgear required, mounted in the enclosure, tested, and ready for the linemen to hook up at the job site. All we would need from the utility would be a one-line electrical drawing, plus their special specifications.

The only "iffy" part of this idea was whether or not our big competitors, knowing we were moving up fast nationally in the sale of enclosures, would sell us their electrical switchgear components. It turned out to be no problem. This was another instance where a good credit record combined with a good reputation as a supplier saved the day. We were eventually able to purchase components of electrical equipment from just about every major U.S. manufacturer. Classified as an original equipment manufacturer, we could not resell the components separately, just as part of our switchgear.

Our switchgear packaging approach was a winner. Not only did WPP realize substantial increases in sales volume, but some of the manufacturers who furnished us components also realized sales increases. We did need to be careful to pay the manufacturer's supply invoices on their terms, some as tight as net ten days.

The switchgear program proved to be another example of the ability of small manufacturers to compete with giant national corporations. The large company was organized around their standard products. Any request for something special usually either was rejected or involved higher pricing and long deliveries. This fact presented a niche opening for WPP. We were determined to exploit this niche and to do it right. We made shop drawings of each new switchgear arrangement ordered by our customers. Each drawing included a bill of material, with source and price of all items listed, and later entered into our computer. Eventually the drawing file grew to several hundred. As a result, what was special order to other manufacturers became standard for our company. We could price a new inquiry in minutes. Once an order was received, it would be in our production schedule the next day. We were told at one point that our company was the leader nationally in the supply of pad-mounted switchgear.

We were careful to comply with all applicable national standards. All switchgear was tested electrically, and for ease of operation, before leaving our plant. In fact, all manufacturers tried to design their equipment to protect the operating lineman.

The lineman's job was one of constant exposure to injury. Some deaths from accidental contact were reported annually, so all manufacturers tried to make operating safety priority number one. However, sometimes accidents did happen.

A case in point was an event that took place in Taos, New Mexico, in the service area of Kit Carson Electric Cooperative. The Taos Indian Village had refused electric service from the Coop for years. Their reason was that the village was holy ground—the oldest continually occupied village in the U.S. Power poles and wires would not fit into their religious area. However, our enclosures resembled in shape their outdoor beehive-type ovens used to bake bread. So, if the wires were run underground, and the transformers were in our fiberglass enclosures, they would accept power from the Coop.

A big celebration was held at Taos at the completion of the electric power project. Joan and I were invited to attend, along with top political, REA, and Indian officials. There were lots of speeches from the flatbed truck that served as a stage, along with Indian dances, and more speeches. We received many compliments about how nicely the enclosures blended into the area.

A couple of years later, we were advised that we were being sued by a lineman who had been injured while involved in a switching procedure in one of our enclosures at Taos. This was the very first time we had been notified of a product liability suit.

The enclosure had a General Electric transformer in it, protected by a McGraw-Edison fused disconnect switch. All three companies were being sued. The total amount was in seven figures. A trial was demanded at Taos.

The accident happened on an election day. The line crew had the afternoon off to vote. The crew had stand-by duty that night and received a trouble call—lights were out. The crew opened the enclosure door to change fuses, and a lineman fell through the open door, contacting 7,200 volts with his hand. He was badly burned, requiring surgery and leaving him with permanent injuries including a crippled hand.

Depositions taken from the linemen as to their activities leading up to the injury did not ring true to me. The injured lineman was a fourteen-year veteran. If he had normally acted as carelessly as the deposition indicated, he could not have survived that long as a lineman. I asked the insurance attorneys to press for details, and to question whether the men had been drinking or using drugs. The crew swore they were free of drugs and alcohol. The hospital had not checked the injured lineman for drugs or alcohol.

The fact the lineman was not complying with industry operating safety procedures would hardly sway a jury, not against wealthy insurance companies. We were insured up in the seven-figure area, but our reputation as a manufacturer of safe pad-mounted switchgear would be tainted by a single injury loss. In addition to our loss of standing in the industry, an injury loss would cause our insurance premiums to shoot up through the roof, provided Tom Galt could find a company willing to sell us insurance.

It was not one of the high-priced investigators that broke the case. It was a paralegal assistant attorney who thought it might be worthwhile to check out the ambulance crew that answered the call that night. The ambulance nurse who was involved was located and questioned. She was a veteran ambulance nurse, and could tell the injured man had been drinking beer, probably a lot.

Here is what we were told actually happened. The line crew had the afternoon off to vote. It was their turn for trouble call duty that night, but they said most trouble calls could wait until the next day. The crew hit the beer pretty heavily after voting, then they all went home. When the trouble call came in, the injured lineman, the acting foreman, drove around to pick up the crew in the line truck, then went to the outage.

As for the linemen's sworn depositions, it was quite natural for a line crew to protect their buddy. They worked around danger every day, and each man watched out for the safety of others in the crew. If they admitted they had been drinking all afternoon, they would lose their jobs. Finally, they wanted their buddy to get a nice big insurance pay-off. The hospital care had been paid by Workers' Compensation Insurance.

We were told the insurance companies representing the three manufacturers contributed to a fund sufficient to reimburse Workers' Compensation for the hospital costs, which ended our involvement in the lawsuit.

The Taos accident diverted our attention for a few weeks from our important national marketing program. We were well along in assigning manufacturer's reps to the various territories. Our next step would be to participate in electrical trade shows, placing our products on display.

Trade shows provided a forum for manufacturers to show off their latest developments in power distribution equipment to their industry, as well as the opportunity to attend various scheduled engineering conferences. Perhaps the largest and best trade show in the electrical industry at that time was a biennial meeting sponsored by the Institute of Electronic and Electrical Engineers. The show rotated among major cities, such as Dallas, Los Angeles, and Chicago. Electric utility people in management, engineering, and operating departments attended from utilities all over the world for the four- or five-day program.

Papers were presented by authorities on a wide range of topics to those attending sessions during the show. A large area was set aside for display booths. The cost of a ten-by-ten-foot booth was up in the four figures, but the real cost was in manning the booth, sometimes for ten hours a day, which required a minimum of two people. Add to this the cost of transportation of people and equipment from factory to show and return, plus hotel and living expenses, and it raised the question—was it worth it?

Yes, it certainly was. If a person had a product or service he wished to sell nationally or worldwide, the trade show was the most effective way to get it before the public. Potential customers from all over the world would stroll by the booth. Those who were interested would stop and usually ask a lot of questions as they picked up the literature. Because of application questions, the booth had to be manned by people who knew all the answers.

Many of our most valuable contacts were made at our display booth. In addition to electric utility people from all over, we were able to visit with sales reps out looking for another product line to sell. We met and visited with executives of competitive companies who liked to check out our products, and we in turn would check out theirs. We had the opportunity to meet with utility executives from Saudi Arabia, the Republic of China, and Nigeria, which resulted in promises of substantial future business in those countries.

We could not make sales to customers directly from the booth, but we could prepare a list of potential customers' names and and addresses. Those who asked for quotations of price and delivery for this or that product could be sent the information after our return home.

The visitors to our booth asked all kinds of questions. Most of the questions were asked by knowledgeable people and made a lot of sense. But then there were also strange questions too. Some we could recognize as ideas planted by our competitors, such as "What is the possibility of your enclosure catching fire?" or "How much of an impact would it take to break a hole in your enclosure?"

One REA manager was considering using our transformer enclosure inside the fence of a cattle pasture. "What would happen if cattle leaned up against the enclosure to scratch?" he asked.

"Nothing."

"All right then, what would happen to the enclosure if a big bull charged it and hit it right in the door area?"

"Probably break it all to hell!"

But then we reviewed for the manager our own impact test and burn test procedures, so that the customer could make his own application judgements.

However, the two features our enclosures had over competition was their sleek appearance, and the guarantee they would not rust. The fiberglass resin was organic, a by-product of the petroleum refining process. Sometimes we had to give written guarantees to engineers that we would replace our enclosures free of charge if they should rust within twenty-five years.

In countries like Taiwan and Saudi Arabia, for example, rust was an ever present problem, because of airborne contaminants. Both these countries routed their people by our booth, to invite me to visit and talk to groups of engineers about our fiberglass enclosure program. This I was happy to do, and I made many more visits in following years, resulting in substantial continuing business.

My interest in export business began with an article in a trade publication. The author recommended that U.S. manufacturers develop an export program and set a goal for export sales of 20 percent of total sales. A strong, planned export program tended to level out factory order input. The U.S. economy was cyclical. In periods of recession in the United States, foreign economies were usually strong, allowing foreign orders to help keep our factories going with jobs for key personnel.

After becoming convinced that WPP should look into the possibilities of an export program, we began to seek a place to start. The state of Oregon, like many other states, had a Department of Economic Development. This proved to be a good source of foreign trade information.

The U.S. Department of Commerce also had offices in our major cities, and their people were also extremely helpful. Here I found lists of all U.S.embassy and consulate offices around the world, with their current officers, addresses, and telephone numbers.

One very helpful service of the Department of Commerce was their sending announcements of new products to their overseas offices. They would send photos and write-ups to all offices for a minimal fee. Their overseas offices would then include a copy of our new product write-up and photo in their local trade news publications. This was a good method of attracting foreign inquiries, and the cost was very low.

Once I was convinced I had products that could be sold overseas, my next objective was to locate agents, required in most countries to represent foreigners doing business there. I was advised first to write to the embassy or consulate in the country I wished to visit, advising of my plans, including complete descriptive data of my products, with my date of arrival and departure clearly stated. I was advised also to ask their assistance in setting up conferences at the embassy or consulate with agents or prospective customers.

After visiting a few consulates, I could see they were indeed busy places. They were usually manned by an officer in charge and several local native trade specialists, who wanted to do all they could to help. They knew the local trade practices, how to go about introducing Americans to management people, and so forth. Therefore, it was necessary to give their commercial departments at least thirty days notice before scheduled arrival.

Some American businessmen wrote off foreign business because they could not speak a foreign language, or because they were afraid to ship products overseas for fear they never would be paid. Some knew of other businessmen who lost money in export business. This could surely happen if a person did not plan carefully.

Regarding the foreign language problem, the foreign businessman really appreciated the American who could speak his language. However, as a practical matter, English was spoken or understood by most businessmen and government people. Unless you were entirely fluent in the foreign language, you were better off to stick with English. I never had any trouble making my way around foreign countries using English, and a little common sense now and then.

We were interested in foreign trade only to make money, not to take a chance of losing money. The way we made sure we would get paid the price that we and our foreign customer agreed on was to require the customer to file a letter of credit, along with a copy of the purchase order made out to our company, and to forward them to our local bank. We made sure all of this took place before shipping anything overseas. The letter of credit guaranteed our payment in full, if the products we were to ship and invoice agreed completely with the letter of credit. We actually received our cash payment from the bank within a couple of days after shipment.

Some foreign businessmen complained about doing business on a letter of credit basis. Some acted as if we were questioning their integrity by requiring such a procedure. I told them, "Hey, it's not our fault, it's our bankers who absolutely insist on it, and we cannot afford to make them unhappy." This approach seemed to work quite well.

If we had a foreign customer who simply could not come up with a letter of credit, this would tip us off that his credit was not good. If his bank would not take a chance on him paying his bill, why should we? We were much better off to write off that type of account and start looking elsewhere. (We also used the letter of credit when selling to domestic customers who had shaky credit reports.)

We reached our goal of export trade equaling 20 percent of our total sales volume within two years, but because of improved profit margins and prompt letter of credit payments, our export trade represented more than 20 percent of our overall gross profit. We never lost money on an export shipment.

In our dealings with electric utilities on the export market, I found it necessary for me, as president, to personally visit officials of the foreign utility to assure them we would treat their account with the same level of service we accorded domestic utility accounts. Also, our policy was to build an ongoing export trade as a permanent division of our marketing effort. This assurance to export customers was necessary because in past years some American manufacturers would make big delivery promises, but let export shipments slide when domestic sales picked up.

"A handshake and a promise, man to man, is better than a handful of written delivery promises," one foreign executive told me.

I had great success with a slide program in dealing with foreign customers. First, we purchased a good 35-millimeter camera, then made sure our pictures were graphic. To demonstrate impact resistance of our enclosures, we had slides showing Bob Foster, our superintendent, swinging an eight-pound sledgehammer against the side of an enclosure. To demonstrate enclosure roof strength, we chose a large enclosure, and had as many men of the shop crew as could fit standing on the roof (see Plate 11). The fire retardant aspect was dramatized in slides showing Bob holding a torch flame against a sample, and the flame going out when the torch was removed. These slides were fully understood, whether the engineers in the audience were Nigerian, Chinese, Arab, or English.

Our slides covered switchgear manufacturing and test procedures, and illustrations of a variety of installations in a cross section of electric utilities around the world. The program included live narration and question periods—a very effective sales tool.

Our very active export marketing effort resulted in our being named Oregon Exporter of the Year in May 1984, and being invited to participate in various conferences and committees. The most interesting export-aligned committee, in my opinion, was the International Trade Advisory Committee to the Oregon Department of Economic Development, International Trade Division. We had committee members in the import/export business, brokers, manufacturers, unions, shipping, a university president and others, all contributing time and effort to monthly meetings.

Doug Frengle, manager of the International Trade Division, and his staff participated in the meetings. It was my pleasure to chair the advisory committee. Our monthly meetings were both informative and interesting, with all committee members contributing.

Early in 1984, Oregon governor Vic Atiyeh scheduled a trade mission to the Middle East. I was invited to join the mission because of our trade experience in Saudi Arabia. Our two-term governor, born in Syria, was a successful local businessman who operated an Oriental rug business established by his family in Portland in 1900. The trade mission included four businessmen, a crew from a local TV station, a state police bodyguard, and the governor's cousin Sammy, a rug merchant, who would act as our interpreter. The governor would be the ideal international trade promoter for our state. His smooth, pleasant approach, combined with his knowledge of business practices and procedures, both domestic and abroad, resulted in our group being treated like royalty.

Our mission visited Riyadh, Jeddah, and Daharan in Saudi Arabia, as well as Cairo, Egypt. At every stop in Saudi Arabia, we were entertained at elaborate luncheons and dinners, usually held in palatial residences of Saudi Arabian royalty. We were always greeted at the entrance to the residence by a receiving line, which included the owner, usually a prince, along with Saudi government aides and local officials. We had an interchange of ideas and business discussions over copious amounts of meats, fruits, and vegetables. (Alcohol is prohibited in Saudi Arabia.)

Governor Atiyeh would ask the businessmen at every stop to tell him what he could do for us there. In my case, I had already visited, on past trips, the officials involved in electric power distribution, and we were already doing business across the country. But I did want to meet the very top officer in the kingdom in the field of electricity, the minister of electricity, a member of the king's cabinet.

Throughout my career as a factory rep and a manufacturer, I made courtesy calls (not sales calls) every few months on the presidents of the companies I dealt with—electric utilities and others. These visits proved to be very helpful in overall customer-supplier relations.

The governor arranged the meeting. Along with a Saudi interpreter, the governor and I were ushered into an impressive office complex. The minister of electricity was seated at his massive desk, dressed in the traditional Saudi garments—white robe with white headcloth held in place by a colored headband. He was engrossed in reading some printed matter when we entered, nodded to us when introduced by the interpreter, and continued his reading. The governor, addressing both the minister and the interpreter, gave one of his excellent but brief speeches.

When it was my turn to speak, my message was one of appreciation of his electrical officials who allowed my company to furnish his government electrical power distribution switchgear, vital to much of their Daharan-area oil production, and in their western province, one of their largest military installations. I finished and waited for the interpreter to relay my message.

Instead the minister looked up and said, "Hey, how are the Trailblazers doing?"

After we recovered our poise and filled him in on the current Trailblazers scoop, we had a pleasant visit.

The minister disclosed that he had attended Portland State University for two years, and had followed our NBA basketball team closely. After continuing his education at other American universities, he often called the Portland newspaper for scores of important Trailblazer games.

We were interested to know why the minister chose Portland State for his two-year enrollment. He explained that years earlier a young Saudi visited Portland, received a warm welcome from residents and faculty at Portland State, and enrolled. He had an excellent two-year course of study and returned to Saudi Arabia to tell everyone about it. Since then, hundreds of other Saudi Arabians have attended Portland State University. The minister continued to sing the praises of Portland, and noted that we Oregonians had a business advantage in Saudi Arabia. "The Saudis know you, your culture, your business policies, and in general, speak your language," he said.

After spending several days in Saudi Arabia, the mission checked into a hotel in Cairo, Egypt. We had good meetings with our embassy personnel and made some business calls, but we were not encouraged with business prospects in Egypt in the near future. One official told us they had no money to spend on public works.

We were told that they depend on the two billion dollars the United States sends them annually for the very basics—water, sewer, and so forth. Other countries also contribute funds for their necessary services. He suggested I visit the consulate at Alexandria before leaving Egypt.

The governor had an appointment to visit with President Mubarak, scheduled for five minutes. A few of our group went along with Governor Atiyeh, hoping to get a sight of the president, but we were directed to seats outside his office while the governor and president visited. The governor said they hit it off very well and had a wide-ranging discussion for thirty minutes.

Some off us took a few hours off for a tour of the Pyramids and the Sphinx. We lacked time to visit other points of interest in the Cairo area. We even turned down an invitation for a cruise on the Nile. Cairo's streets and buildings, and the airport, seemed badly in need of maintenance.

The trade mission was completed in Cairo, but the party had plans to accompany the governor to Syria for a homecoming ceremony. My plans were to leave the group after our breakfast meeting, hire a car and driver, and head down the Nile to Alexandria for a visit with our consulate to learn the details of an upcoming big project.

Alexandria was a very impressive, interesting city. Our drive back to Cairo was memorable in that the brick wall of a four-story building collapsed on the sidewalk in downtown Cairo, right beside our car while we were stalled in traffic. No one was hurt, but the event did nothing to help my feelings of insecurity while walking the streets of Cairo.

18

Litigation and Patent Procedures

It was now back to business after a memorable trip with Governor Atiyeh's Middle East Trade Mission. Things were happening in our business while we were traveling the Middle East. Our hard-working salesman, Dave Skeans, who pioneered the introduction of our fiberglass enclosures by hauling a trailer of our products around the country behind his car, had occasion to visit an electric utility in Florida. During the discussion he was shown a newsletter a customer had received in the mail from one of the largest American electrical manufacturers, and our principal competitor in the switchgear enclosure market. The newsletter seemed to be devoted primarily to the destruction of Western Power Products as a switchgear enclosure competitor.

The copy included several outright lies about our company and our products and some mislabeled photos. It reflected much of the misinformation then being circulated among the electric utilities by their salesmen nationally. Our marketing people were kept busy denying the false claims being circulated by an otherwise reputable national manufacturer.

I called a meeting of our board of directors to discuss the newsletter. It was my strong feeling it was necessary to challenge the competitor without delay. We knew they had recently completed a new plant to mass-produce steel equipment enclosures. We also had trade information indicating we were very close to overtaking the steel competitor in dollar volume of enclosure sales. Apparently the pressure was on their sales and marketing people to take the steam out of our company.

Our board agreed the only course to follow was to first ask the company to cease and desist, and for them to retract the statements in their newsletter. We asked our corporate secretary, attorney Don McEwen, to contact the appropriate management individual in the competitor's company to discuss the problem.

"I've been in contact with their general counsel, who advised me they simply don't have time to investigate claims of this type. He also said he would take no further action regarding our complaint," Don reported a few days later.

With our competitor's attitude so eloquently stated, we could expect a continuation of their national effort to discredit us with their program of outright lies. We had a choice to make. Accordingly, the board voted to instruct the secretary to file suit against our large and wealthy competitor for a seven-figure dollar amount, with a jury trial to be scheduled in Portland.

Suddenly their general counsel was able to find time to investigate the complaint. The lawsuit really attracted his attention. Before long, their management was in contact with Don. Apparently they were not aware of the tactic their marketing department had employed against WPP. One of their top officials asked for a private meeting with me in Portland to discuss the overall problem, with no attorneys present, just the two of us. This arrangement was fine with me. We were not in the lawsuit business. We simply wanted to pursue our business without their libelous interference.

At the private meeting, we spent several hours in a Portland hotel room. Neither wanted a lawsuit. We searched for and found a way to settle our dispute out of court. The settlement included a sum of money to WPP to cover our legal expenses, and a firm guarantee that nothing like the past senseless marketing program would ever happen again. Personnel responsible for the newsletter content would be changed upon his return to his headquarters. Several changes in his marketing personnel were indeed publicly announced a week later. Further, if we were to become aware of any of their salespeople making false statements against our company, I was to call him directly, and that person would be fired. I was convinced of his determination to put an end to the entire ugly affair.

We shook hands on the deal. The million-dollar lawsuit was discontinued, much to the relief of everyone involved. As far as I know, no one in our company ever again encountered problems of unfair competition with this company.

Some people asked why we settled for such a small dollar amount from such a wealthy company. What we really wanted was to get this powerful national competitor off our back. We were sure we could beat them in the marketplace if we were playing on a level field. We did not want to spend the next several months going through the time-consuming nuisance of depositions and interrogatories for the opposing attorneys to use in the trial. And then, of course, it would have been difficult to prove to what extent we had been damaged financially, so that any kind of cash settlement could have been resolved.

We looked on this lawsuit as another instance of the value of patent protection. The fastest, least expensive way for our competitor to get rid of our challenge to their switchgear enclosure market would have been to copy our fiberglass enclosure and our methods of installing switchgear. But they knew that we would hit them with a patent infringement suit if they copied our product line, so the only other solution their marketing people could come up with, unfortunately, was to slander our product. Thanks to the guidance of our patent attorney and the research of our staff, the resulting design patent once again saved the product line.

We all knew it was wrong (and illegal) for several competitors to get together and agree to sell a similar product for the same or a fixed price. So, to increase sales, manufacturers sometimes cut prices, which meant a sacrifice of quality, customer service, or profit margin. When one company started cutting, others usually followed. This everyday rat race took much of the fun and profit out

188 Two Bills From Boston

of manufacturing. However, with adequate patent protection, one was free to produce a top-quality product to sell at a reasonable price level, sufficient to realize a profit and to earn a return on investment. Then, if one did a proper job of selling against competitive items on the market, the fun and excitement of true competition began.

I had quite a few people question me about patent procedures: "I have a great idea—how should I proceed, and what does it cost?"

To these wannabe inventors, my advice generally was: "To begin with, I don't want to hear any of the details of your special invention. My suggestion is to proceed as I did with my first product development. First, sketch your product and write in detail the features you hope can be patented. The more descriptive the detail, the better. Then go to a large city public library and scan through the list of products similar to yours that have been patented. If you find something the same or similar to yours that has been patented or in use previously, it is best to forget it. You can only patent that which is novel, something with new features.

"If the library search turns up nothing similar, the next step would be to discuss your idea with a patent attorney, preferably a person who deals exclusively in patent law. Patent attorneys can be trusted to keep patent details confidential, except to U.S. Patent Office employees. If the attorney agrees there is a good chance the item can be patented, he may suggest as a first step an arrangement with a correspondent attorney in Washington, D.C., for the preliminary search through the patent files. This correspondent would then furnish your attorney copies of patents found to be close to your idea. You should ask the patent attorney for estimates of the various patent application costs during your first meeting."

Although most of my contacts have been with only one top-rated patent attorney, Eugene Eckleman, I have told those who have asked how to take the important first steps from idea to patent application, as follows:

If the correspondent patent attorney in Washington, D.C., finds no conflicting patents, the next step is for the local patent attorney to prepare a formal patent application. Included are drawings prepared by a specially trained patent draftsman, as required by the patent office, along with the special "patent talk" required in the description and explanation of functional parts of the product. Once the application is filed, the inventor can begin producing the product if he wishes to, and applying the label "Patent Applied For" to each item and all advertising. During the year-long patent approval process, no one outside the patent office has access to the information in the inventor's application.

If all goes well and the application is approved, the inventor receives a certificate from the patent office, and documents containing drawings and description of the product, along with the assigned patent number and the approval date.

People in business may apply the patent immediately, as we have done. Some inventors who are employees in a business often sign over patent rights to their employer, particularly if the inventor has worked on development of the product during company time. And some people who have had a good idea have done something about it on their own time, like Joe Williams and Perry Landsom.

It is my opinion the very best procedure for the inventor is to seriously consider manufacturing the patented product himself, maintaining complete control. This is the ideal. This is where the most financial benefits and personal satisfaction can be derived from the patent process. Not everyone, however, is prepared to undertake a manufacturing/marketing program. This would suggest a sale of patent rights to others.

In the case of Perry Landsom and Joe Williams and their tensioning brake mentioned earlier, we agreed to manufacture the tensioner, paying them a set royalty on every tensioner sold. The agreement was among good friends. All we had to go forward with was a memo of understanding and a handshake. I could not recommend this procedure to others, however. There are lots of loopholes and pitfalls in agreements between inventors and manufacturers. There seem to be a lot more bad experiences in this area than good ones.

After determining where the product could be marketed, I would recommend finding an attorney with experience in inventor/manufacturer agreements. This is a tricky area. A person needs legal advice before signing any patent release forms with a manufacturer.

I have always considered the U.S. patent process a great privilege, a means for the average person to use his imagination in ways to make things better in the world, and in the process to improve himself economically. It certainly has worked for me for sixteen U.S. and four Canadian patents, plus three copyrighted trade names.

19

Consolidation of Plants and Functions

By the early 1970s the company was again running short of manufacturing capacity. Switchgear enclosures were moving very well, particularly in the southeastern United States. We determined in late 1972 that about 50 percent of our shipments were east of the Rocky Mountains, mostly to Georgia and Florida. The cost of freight to our eastern markets averaged 10 percent of the selling price, versus 4 percent in western markets.

This started us thinking of an eastern plant. The eastern demand center for our products was in Georgia, so we considered the Atlanta area. In discussing our needs with friends at Georgia Power, we were assured that the state of Georgia would be very interested in assisting us to find a location. They would set up a conference for us with the Georgia Department of Economic Development.

As a possibility, we chose a modern industrial building in the small town of Villa Rica, west of Atlanta. The rent was reasonable and the lease was for five years.

The state offered to pretrain our local employees at no cost to us, using videotapes of our manufacturing process. Everything seemed to go together well. We signed a lease to begin in thirty days, to allow time to equip the plant. We would use the plant to test a new production method we were working on, involving movement of our heavy, bulky fiberglass molds from station to station, to reduce labor and increase production. Also, we would use a new plant production line layout designed to reduce nonproductive labor.

We hired a man who had a long career in engineering and manufacturing with a major electrical company. He was looking for a change of jobs and was excited about managing our new plant. Our son Larry had recently completed college and was looking for a management challenge, so he became the office manager.

We were determined to try our idea for moving the heavy molds between work stations using a monorail system. The roof structure of the building was not strong enough to support the loaded monorail, so we designed a bridge structure consisting of four-inch steel pipes as side vertical supports, and a crossbeam with the monorail secured beneath it.

It was necessary for the monorail to remain level throughout the uneven floor surface. To accomplish this, we carefully laid out the location of each support structure, identified each with a number, and checked and recorded the floor elevation with a transit at each structure location.

With this data in hand, we were able to fabricate each structure and the monorail in our Portland plant and ship it to Villa Rica for installation by our crew. It worked beautifully. Our largest molds, which required three or four men to move in older plants, could now be easily moved by a child.

We agreed to lease the plant in February 1973 and were in production in July 1973. It was a great new plant, but with new problems. The shop employees, trained by the state of Georgia using our materials and methods, did not turn out too well. Many could not make it to work every morning. Some could not last the eight-hour work day. Many others just quit after a few days. So we had to temporarily transfer key employees from Portland to hire and train employees for Villa Rica.

We had the Villa Rica plant manager in to our Clackamas fiberglass plant for two weeks to observe and learn the production and inspection details of fiberglass enclosure production. He was provided with a budget for operating the Villa Rica plant, and a monthly production goal. He was to send monthly production reports to our Portland office. After some months of operation, we noticed his inventory building up far beyond what it should have been.

I asked our employee Jim Coon, who was in the east on business, to go by the Villa Rica plant and check why the inventory was so large. His telephone call gave me the bad news.

Jim was very upset and said the large inventory had surface blemishes and was mostly not salable. Improper production methods resulted in unacceptable appearance on the outer surfaces of the enclosures. The repair procedure was labor-intensive and expensive. Thousands of dollars would have to be spent to make the inventory salable.

The plant manager's production reports were inaccurate and misleading. His management and inspection record was unsatisfactory, so we had to let him go. We then set a new course for the Villa Rica plant and promoted Larry to take over as plant manager. He set up a repair program for the unsatisfactory enclosures, and retrained the crew in lay-up and inspection procedures. He developed a new skin-coat process that largely eliminated the cause of the defects.

The Villa Rica plant under Larry's management became profitable, and it generally remained profitable during the remainder of the lease period. When it came time to close the plant, Larry took great pains to dismantle the monorail for shipment back to Portland, along with all molds, machinery and equipment, leaving a clean building.

The Villa Rica plant did relieve the production capacity problems at the Clackamas plant and gave us some breathing room to address the overall production problem. The Clackamas plant lease would be up in 1974. The building was adequate when we leased it, but now it was inadequate. What we needed was a new building designed for our production needs.

It was time to look around for potential new plant sites outside the city of Portland. My search began with a conference with friends at Pacific Power & Light Company. Their district managers were usually aware of the cities that were interested in attracting new business. Calling on a few cities on my own, it seemed that Portland was the only city that had problems with fiberglass manufacturing plants. All the other cities I contacted were anxious to attract a steady payroll of over $1 million per year. Payroll dollars would go directly to the economy of the area, from the marketplace to storekeepers, dentists, attorneys, and so forth. Some offered incentives for us to move to their city.

I soon received a phone call from a Pacific Power & Light district manager, Hank Hurlbert, at Hood River, a city approximately sixty miles east of Portland on the Columbia River, in the center of the Cascade Mountain Range. Hank invited me to a luncheon with the local Port Commission. He said the commissioners were eager to discuss the possibility of our relocating to Hood River.

The meeting went well. The objective of the Port was to have a manufacturing payroll to complement the basic fruit orchard and timber industries already in the city. These community leaders understood the value of independent business payrolls to their local economy. There were no special business taxes.

Meanwhile, the company continued to grow. Our office staff required more and more space. Rather than build more space, we contracted a data processing firm to handle our payroll. The following two months involved constant problems with the data processing outfit, so we were finally forced to take the fearful step of purchasing our own computer. We hired temporary help to reorganize our office procedures to suit the computer and to train our office staff for computer operations.

While the port negotiations were going on, so was our product development program. The development that interested me most was in the power distribution business. Power distribution substations had been part of our basic activity since the very beginning of the company. Few real improvements in substation design had been made in the industry for decades. What started me thinking seriously about the need for a new design was a report issued to electric utilities analyzing accidents the industry had reported during the previous year.

The report segregated injuries into work areas. The number of fatalities in power distribution substations was hard to believe, and most were the result of accidental contact during routine operations. Even more surprising, the accidents were usually to older employees with ten to fifteen years experience—people who knew all about risk around high voltage. Often the injured employees had been conducting routine maintenance operations, frequently in inclement weather or darkness, and often under time pressure.

I developed a means of substantially reducing the possibility of accidental contact injuries by placing all apparatus and switchgear located in the dangerous secondary (lower voltage) side of a substation into individual fiberglass enclosures. We used underground cables (instead of exposed conductors) to interconnect the various switchgear and outgoing circuits. The new design worked out very well. Not only was it an advance in safety, by completely eliminating the possibility of accidental contact with overhead conductors, but it substantially reduced the possibility of outages caused by vandals and storm damage. The appearance of a power distribution substation also was greatly enhanced. The new substation design would be ideal for suburban areas where residential development outside the city suburbs demanded more substation capacity.

A check of the patent files listed only one substation patent, an award to Westinghouse Electric Company for an urban substation design. Their design occupied a minimum of ground level surface area but increased in height as additional capacity was required. I filed a patent application for our suburban version and also applied for copyright approval of the name "Western Suburban." Both applications were approved. Brisk sales by the dozens followed, from Maine to Alaska to New Mexico. As far as we knew, there never was a report of an accidental contact injury in a Western Suburban substation.

After advising the Hood River Port Commission that the bond market would not be suitable to finance our project, there was a delay of some weeks in negotiations. The next contact with the Port was a phone call from Dallas Dusenberry, the manager.

"There may be some other way than a bond issue to finance the building. Would you please give us a firm dollar amount you would need to finance the building?" he asked.

We had developed general arrangement drawings for a building, and now it would be necessary to fill in the details. We asked Jerry Schicht, a general contractor who had a good reputation for building construction in Hood River to give us a firm price quotation.

The six-figure amount seemed reasonable to us and to the Port, so a deal was finally at hand. We selected a choice location on the Columbia River waterfront for the four-acre plot for the building, plus a five-year option for an adjacent plot for expansion.

The financial terms were reasonable, allowing us a six-month move-in-and-settling period after completion of construction before our first monthly payment of principal and interest was due. However, we strongly objected to the fact the Port insisted on maintaining title to the land, which they expected to lease at a set monthly rate for twenty years. After twenty years, our building mortgage would be paid off, but the Port would own the land. The land argument went for weeks.

After much discussion and analysis, we decided to go ahead on the Port's terms. Our reasoning in accepting the land lease was that our payroll would be leverage to induce the Port to extend the land lease on favorable terms. If the Port chose to be unreasonable, we could sell or dismantle our building and move elsewhere. The cost of servicing the building loan was far less than rent for an equivalent building. Any capital gain we might receive for the building after twenty years would be a plus. For the twenty-year lease period, the Port would be paying property tax on the four acres of expensive waterfront property.

Once the groundbreaking ceremony was behind us, the building construction program proceeded on schedule. Our energetic general contractor, Jerry, scheduled the subcontractors, and hovered over them like a mother hen. We chose a Butler steel building, with special reinforcing in the roof structure to support our monorail system plus the anticipated maximum snow load.

We decided to install the systems that were especially important to our manufacturing process with our own shop crew. Our superintendent, Bob Foster, supervised the installation of the monorail system. Next in line for Bob was the heating system for our shops. The fiberglass shop was heated by unit gas heaters, which were installed on a firewall outside the fiberglass shop, with the heat ducted into the work area. The balance of the shop area and warehouse was heated by a highly efficient gas-fired system called CO-RAY-VAC, which proved to be outstanding and trouble free.

The balance of the plant went together easily. Bob also supervised the move, starting with our offices, then the Clackamas plant, followed by the Portland plant. At last, we could consolidate all our manufacturing operations, along with our office operations, in one building. We would review our costs and production capacity over the following months before making a decision on closing the Atlanta plant.

Our office manager, John Benedetti, and our bookkeeper, Ina Alford, could not move with us to Hood River owing to family reasons. We were fortunate to find highly qualified replacements in the Hood River area for our important office positions.

Joy Vital, a woman strong in business credentials, took over as office manager/bookkeeper. Our daughter Mary moved to Hood River and took over the critical job of cost accountant. Donna Hukari, starting as receptionist, grew into various office positions and finally became secretary for my office and the engineering department.

All in all, 1975 was a very busy year. We signed our agreement with the Port in February. We moved into the new plant during August, September and October. Joan and I purchased a home in Hood River. I started my term as President of Northwest Electric Light and Power Association, and Joan took over the various women's social activities associated with the NELPA meetings. However, during the year, we managed to keep our business moving along without interruption. We found the cost of the move, using entirely our own people, exceeded the estimated $100,000.

The first few months of operations in our new plant were heavily involved in breaking in new office, shop, and fiberglass plant employees. The consolidation of fiberglass plant and machine shops made a huge difference in our productivity and sharply reduced our costs—so much so that we made the decision to gradually phase out our Villa Rica plant.

In Hood River, we continued our practice of bringing in an independent accounting firm to conduct our annual audit, which included oversight and check of our annual shop and warehouse inventory count. One reason for the inventory count was to satisfy our management that our year-end financial statements were accurate; another reason was to convince the Internal Revenue Service that we were presenting them accurate year-end financial numbers.

The outside accounting firm who conducted our first audit after moving into the new building was the firm of Harold Youal & Associates. A CPA member of the firm, Lynn Beier, was involved in the audit. Some time after the audit, we recognized the need to add a CPA to our staff to perform the duties of a comptroller. We were growing fast, computerizing many of our procedures, and we needed help. We started looking for a sharp, full time CPA. The next time Lynn Beier was at the plant, I asked him if he knew of any CPA who might be interested in joining our company.

Lynn indicated he might be interested, having looked over our corporate structure very carefully during his audit. After some discussions, and the assurance that corporate stock would be available for him, Lynn made the decision to join the company in March 1976.

We had not realized how much we needed a person of his talents as a comptroller until he took over management of all accounting, bookkeeping, quotations, and banking. Lynn's detailed monthly operating statements, which he would place on my desk during the first week of the following month, were extremely valuable to me in doing my job as president.

When we cleared out the Portland property, we placed it on the market through a large realtor. Our asking price was $425,000. The property was slow to sell. A year went by before a buyer appeared who was willing to pay $390,000. We agreed to sell at the reduced price, which was after all, a fair profit over the $200,000 we had paid for the property seven years earlier.

Sale of the Portland property underlined the importance for a growing company to move into ownership of its building head-quarters as soon as possible. Rent money was lost and gone forever, and was subject to increase for a number of reasons. Mortgage payments, however, were much more stable, subject only to tax increases, and the value of the property, if properly located, would increase owing to inflation and area business development.

Our business was founded and grew mainly as a supplier to the electric utility industry. As the electric utility industry went through another of its cyclical dips, we started thinking seriously about other sources of business to supplement the utility business. Many of the larger industrial and commercial contractors, as well as local and federal government agencies, depend on electrical consultants to prepare their plans and specifications for new projects. We decided to let these consultants know how we might be of service to them. We would conduct our own marketing survey.

This would be a marketing survey best handled by our wives. Joan, Debbie Sanguras, and Marg Beier agreed to come to the office part time for survey work. They borrowed telephone books from the local telephone company covering principal cities in the states we had targeted. Then they checked out and listed the consultants, eliminating specialty fields and those other than elec-trical. They called the more promising consultants, telling them what WPP did in design and manufacture of power supply products, and asking if they would like to have our catalog.

The market survey proved to be inexpensive to carry out and was very effective, resulting in a good mailing list of interested consultants. We then had our salesmen follow up with delivery of catalogs, and the opportunity to answer trade questions. Better still, the market surveys resulted in substantial business. We could see that the industrial, commercial, and government markets were many times larger in business potential for our product than the electric utility market. We realized some substantial new business.

Our Hood River plant (see Plate 13) was designed for construction in three phases. Phase one contained sufficient space to consolidate the two Portland area plants and get operations under way. By early 1979, our increased activity demanded more space, so we called in Jerry Schicht to add phase two. This extension provided for a tooling shop, a storage area, a large warehouse, and a loading dock. On the second floor of the new addition we added three offices and a large conference room—all completed in December 1979.

With our new conference room we could now schedule sales meetings for our representatives around the country. There were nearby motels and restaurants, and our international airport was only forty-five minutes away. We invited about a dozen salesmen at a time for a two-day conference. Part of the time would be spent in conference room discussions related to sales of our products. Time also would be spent in our shops, observing our people at work; we encouraged them to ask questions.

Most time and questions were spent on fiberglass enclosures, ranging in size from small service pedestals measuring nine inches square by thirty inches high, to walk-in models ten feet deep, ten feet wide, and ten feet high. The salesmen, reflecting queries from their customers, were always skeptical about manufacturer's claims of product strength and endurance.

We were prepared for this line of questioning. Our superintendent, Bob Foster, would hit the side of an enclosure with a sledgehammer to demonstrate impact resistance. The sledgehammer would bounce back with no damage. The same sledgehammer blow on a competitive steel enclosure along side would leave a large dent or an open seam. The burn demonstration proved the fiberglass material would not support combustion. When the acetylene flame was removed, the resin flame self-extinguished.

Both demonstrations proved our advertising claims to the most skeptical salesmen. One of our principal objectives at sales meetings was to point out the difference between ordinary fiberglass, which was brittle and combustible, and our fiberglass material, identified as Powerglass. Powerglass, our copyright name, was specially compounded for high impact resistance and would not support combustion.

Electric utilities are very particular about the integrity of their high voltage switchgear enclosures because they all have vandalism problems. The vandals were usually a few young people who were curious to find out what was inside the enclosure. They would beat on the roof and sides, try to pry open a door, or force an opening large enough to poke a wire or stick inside. Our goal in design was to maintain the integrity of the enclosure against acts of vandalism, and to reduce the chance of accidental contact by the public with the high voltage equipment inside.

A nother benefit of our new plant, in addition to sales meetings, was the opportunity to review our procedures and to fine-tune our operations. One very important production material we were anxious to review was the resins used in our fiberglass manufacturing. Our largest monthly cash outlay for raw material was to out-of-state resin suppliers. The resins were formulated to our specifications and delivered to us in truckloads of fifty-five-gallon steel drums. The drums were stored in an outdoor area and brought into the plant a drum or two at a time, as a fire precaution.

Manhandling the drums in and out of the plant used production labor and time. Also, as happened in 1979, resin suppliers would play games with us, quoting erratic price and delivery times, when our resin inventory required replacement. Our refusal to accept a price increase could mean the shutdown of the fiberglass shop. Finally, we had no way to check chemical analysis when receiving resin by the barrel.

In addition to doing a first-class job as our comptroller, Lynn Beier liked a challenge, and he took over the resin supply problem. He studied our chemical formula, the reliability of our sources, and vendor's pricing procedures, and visited resin manufacturer's facilities. Lynn recommended we purchase a used tank trailer with a capacity of 4,500 gallons. With our own tank trailer, we could go directly to any manufacturer and purchase resin by the tanker load, or we could have resin delivered to our tanker. This system would allow us to monitor each new resin supply before acceptance to be sure it met our standards. It would also alert our suppliers that we could shop for fair prices and haul our own if need be.

We did purchase a stainless steel tank trailer, and it fit our needs exactly. With the tanker in place outside the building, we piped the resin directly into a holding tank in the lay-up room, where resin temperature could be maintained at a constant level best for production. The monthly savings for resin, labor, and materials was in four figures.

Another area Lynn concentrated on was invoice financing. If we bid on a project, and received a purchase order from our customer for our bid price of say, $100,000, we could borrow an amount from the bank to cover our cost of labor and material, say $75,000. The bank would charge us a rate that changed from time to time, based on the Federal Reserve prime rate plus two points or so over prime. Provided our anticipated profit margin held up where it belonged, we made out well.

In this area of banking, Lynn demonstrated again the value of having a real comptroller aboard. His close management of funds as our chief financial officer resulted in our payment of less and less interest to the bank, month after month, until finally we had sufficient operating capital of our own and could finance all our requirements. There was indeed no substitute for bank financing when our company really needed it, but it was a giant step forward to arrive at a stage of company growth where it was no longer needed. As our vice president and assistant to the president, Lynn was comfortable in wearing many hats in addition to chief financial officer. He represented management in AFL/CIO labor negotiations, internal revenue (IRS) reviews, negotiations for sale of our Portland property, and numerous other special projects.

The basis of our favorable cash flow which allowed Lynn to continually build the financial strength of WPP was the orderly scheduling of production through the plant. Demand for our enclosures, with various types of switchgear installed, continued to grow. Volume for substations also increased monthly. This large variety of products to be shipped every month represented a real challenge to the production manager. His job was to ship enough production every month to pay the fixed costs of production, plus supplier invoices and other variable costs.

We recognized the need for steady, adequate cash flow from the beginning, establishing monthly targets in dollar volume to ship, for each of our product lines. It sounds disarmingly simple to tell the employees what to ship every month and have it happen. However, in real life it takes more—a person with overall production authority to accomplish the meticulous planning and to oversee all details involved. The purchasing and delivery of all manufacturing components, the timely completion of each manufacturing process, the inspection, shipping and customer invoicing—all must go together each and every month.

After operating in our new Hood River plant for a year, our production control continued to be a problem. Shipments every month proceeded as if we had no schedule, either below or above our production goals. Our production manager was probably doing his best, but we had to let him go.

Soon after the departure of our production manager, the Villa Rica plant had been closed, and all its inventory and equipment were shipped to the Hood River plant. Larry Sanguras, the Villa Rica plant manager, had been doing a good job of turning that plant around from a mismanaged financial drain under the previous manager to a profitable operation. We named Larry the production manager of the Hood River plant, giving him responsibility for all customer services, duties he had previously handled at Villa Rica.

With Larry in charge, the new production control required all incoming purchase orders to arrive first at Larry's desk to be analyzed and scheduled. The customer was then notified of the scheduled shipping date. Everyone involved in purchasing, manufacturing, and invoicing knew what was expected of them. As signs of trouble appeared in the scheduling of an order, Larry was notified so that corrective action could be taken. It was amazing to see the difference it made in our monthly billings. Every month became a winner, making Lynn's job easier, and all jobs more secure.

One of Larry's strong points was in customer contacts. Our representatives and customers around the country regularly called the plant for quotations on supply of various products, or to expedite something on order, or just to visit. Larry had the knack of communicating with all who might call, and his knowledge of every aspect of the business kept the company's customer contacts on a friendly and efficient basis.

Just how important Larry's repartee was with our customers would be difficult to gauge, but one good example was his switching pedestal project. He came to see me one day after visiting with one of our representatives on the East Coast. It seemed this rep had told Larry about a competitor's steel switching cabinet designed to be partly buried in the ground, with a lid that opened to provide access for switching elbow disconnects. Elbow disconnects might be described as insulated 15,000-volt disconnect switches attached to the end of an underground electric cable, and designed to be operated with a lineman's hot stick. Larry assured the rep that he would see what could be done about making a sample in fiberglass.

"As you know, we already have standard enclosures suitable for mounting elbow disconnects," I said.

"But this new design would be very low profile, and designed just for elbow disconnects, and guaranteed not to rust below ground," Larry said.

"Well, it seems pretty wild to me, but if you will give me a dimensional sketch, we will kick it around some more," I replied.

So, with Larry's sketch in hand, we decided to make an inexpensive mold for a sample. One challenge was providing the eighteen-inch underground section of the structure base strength enough to withstand the pressure of earth loading. I accomplished this with a sloping elliptical design. Jim Coon worked on the steel mounting for the elbow disconnects, to provide just the right angle for linemen to operate the elbows.

The finished product looked very promising, so much so I loaned my hard hat to our factory salesman, John Chichester, and took his picture with hot stick in hand making like a lineman, doing a switching operation (see Plate 15). The switching pedestals were a hit from the very beginning. They became a favorite around resort areas, golf courses, and other landscaped properties. Before shipping a pedestal, we applied for and were awarded a patent. We long ago lost track of how many thousands of switching pedestals have been sold. This was another product developed by our team approach.

Another energetic member of our management team was Jim Coon. Jim was our resource for standards and practices in the electric utility industry. He was a tireless worker, a stickler on customer service and a good inspector. Jim made sure every switchgear product that left the plant would pass the tests of the electric utility operators. As an ex-lineman who worked his way up the ladder to line foreman in a large electric utility, there was little Jim did not know about utility operations. He started with us as a commission salesman, then advanced to salaried salesman and on to sales manager, and later to vice president and a stockholder.

Jim, Lynn, Larry, and I worked well together as a team. Each team member had an input that was respected by the others. Normally, after a discussion, we all reached the same conclusion.

On the rare occasions where there was not a consensus, the others all joined in with a "let's make it work" attitude. It was the people who made the company—people who were loyal, interested individuals and were willing to work for what they thought to be right. We certainly had some of the best at Western Power Products.

Our weekly staff meetings brought together everyone involved in production—the shop superintendent and foreman, along with shipping, purchasing, engineering, and others, as needed. Monthly production schedules were reviewed on a week-by-week basis. The process paid off in many ways. Here again, everyone took part in the discussion, regardless of rank or seniority.

Our marketing survey indicated that an engineering consulting firm in Atlanta was interested in our products, so, on my next visit to Atlanta, I arranged to visit them. We had a good discussion of our engineering capabilities. They had no current projects that could involve us, but they suggested we contact a group in New York City who were active in contacting major contractors around the world. They offered contractors their service in locating manufacturers who could produce products required for various projects.

The New York group, MIMCO KBK International, was working at that time, with a Korean contractor on a major project slated for Saudi Arabia. The project was to be a military base and required special sizes of housings for a wide assortment of equipment used to back up their electrical system. One-line drawings were available describing the electrical functions required. We were given the opportunity to develop the one-line drawings into arrangement drawings, and to provide details and specifications, with pricing, of equipment we proposed to furnish. We were under way with the drawings in June 1982. Our contact at KBK was Andy Bergesson.

This was to be a very involved project. Our large walk-in enclosures would require steel skid bases, filtered ventilation, equipment to start and control adjacent diesel generators, and equipment to regulate and control outgoing vital electrical circuits. In short, the kind of a job we really enjoyed going after. We completed all detailed drawings by late August, along with our price quotation, which was one of our largest projects to date in total dollar value.

During the next several months we visited with Andy and KBK principals in their New York offices, and Andy visited our plant with two Korean engineers. The approval process, stretching from New York to Korea to Saudi Arabia, was of necessity very slow. However, we were awarded the contract in January 1983. In March we made our first shipments, followed in a few weeks with the balance.

Everyone was pleased with the enclosures and switchgear. We carefully prepared the enclosures for export, covering all units completely to avoid shipping damage. But the stevedores at the Saudi Arabian dock were a bit careless with their forklift trucks, damaging some of the units. Bob Foster, our shop superintendent, gathered tools and repair material and met me in Saudi Arabia. He did a first-class repair job. The Korean crew and Saudi inspectors were happy with Bob's work, and we were reimbursed for our expenses.

Needless to say, we all appreciated the work of our market survey team—our wives Joan, Debbie, and Marg. They found the way, through their phone contacts, not only to our largest contract, but also to many others. Their knowledgeable and friendly approach really paid off in new business.

20

Business Activity—Hood River and Nigeria

A few years before the arrival of the windsurfers made Hood River famous, our company was welcomed to this Columbia Gorge community. We all became involved: Lynn in city government, Larry as a National Guard officer, the women office staff in a sorority, and Joan and I in politics.

The fruit industry employed a large number of Mexicans. They seemed to enjoy harvesting apples and pears, pruning trees, and other orchard work. We noticed a definite animosity between American workers and the Mexicans when we came to town. The Americans complained the Mexicans were taking their jobs. However, visiting with orchard owners disclosed that the Mexicans were at least twice as productive as the American workers.

We experienced a problem finding Americans who would work for any length of time in the fiberglass shop. The odor of styrene, and the itching effect of fiberglass on skin caused problems for many of our original American employees. We tried Mexican workers, starting with two. They worked out so well we hired more Mexicans as openings came up.

The Mexicans seemed to like fiberglass work and many would sing as they worked. They also liked the change from seasonal work in the orchards to our steady year-round work.

We had no problems with the Port of Hood River. We always made our payments on time. The manager and commissioners were friendly, fine people. We had only one slight difference of opinion during my watch. It developed at a Port luncheon where I had been invited as their guest. After the luncheon, one of the commissioners informed me they were going to raise our monthly lease payments to reimburse the Port for an increase they were assessed on county taxes. It seemed our four acres of waterfront property had more than doubled in valuation since we completed our agreement, causing the county to raise the taxes paid by the Port.

We were, of course, sorry to learn of the tax increase the Port would be paying. However, during the yearlong negotiation for the building, the Port advised us their policy was to retain ownership of the land. The agreement was structured accordingly, and signed by both parties. One advantage in leasing the land was we could avoid taxes, if the contract was so structured. Ownership of the land meant paying taxes, plus any tax increases. However, the landowner would ultimately be rewarded by the increase in value.

"No way will we reopen the contract at this late date. Any attempt by the Port to enforce such an increase will mean an appearance in court," I said. The subject was never brought up again.

Back in the early days of the company, my association with Senator Wayne Morse demonstrated to me how important it was for a business owner to make it a point to become acquainted with our representatives in Congress. When the National Federation of Independent Businesses scheduled a national conference in Washington, D.C., to discuss small business problems, Joan and I were members and made plans to attend.

The conference proved to be very worthwhile. Speakers covered many of the problems inherent in the operation of a small business. After an in-depth discussion of legislation pending in Congress which would have an impact on small business, we were urged to spend the afternoon visiting our congressmen to give them the word. Congress was aware of our meeting going on, and that we would be visiting many of them on the stated afternoon.

Joan and I spent most of our time with Oregon senators Bob Packwood and Mark Hatfield. We were graciously received and given plenty of time to impart the small business message. We asked both senators to visit our new plant in Hood River the next time they were in our area, so that we could show them some of the points we were discussing.

Both agreed to visit us. Then to cap the day, in the evening at our hotel we rode up in the elevator with Ronald Reagan and his assistant. It was a lucky chance to have a very short chat with our future president.

Two months after our visit to Washington, Senator Packwood came by the plant. We had very little notice, and the senator had very little time. We toured the plant and had a good discussion, and then he was on his way.

It was eight months later that we heard from Senator Hatfield's office. He planned to visit us the next week and would confirm the day before. This gave us an opportunity to make his visit a local event. We planned a luncheon for a party of twelve to be held in our conference room. Joan volunteered to prepare her special fried chicken, potato salad, and Oregon razor clam chowder, with Hood River apple pie. Our daughter Mary helped with arrangements and made sure everyone had their fill.

The senator arrived on schedule with his long time assistant Gerry Frank. They were near the end of a week-long campaign trip through eastern Oregon. Both looked sort of tired and hungry. Our guest list included the local radio station owner, the local newspaper editor, chairman of the Hood River County commission, a Port commissioner and the Port manager. Lynn Beier and I were hosts.

Conversation during luncheon was lively and interesting. The senator received a good briefing about what one small business means to one small community, and he heard it from the leaders of the community. He also had a report on legislation being considered in Congress at that time. After the last piece of apple pie had disappeared, he started talking about their swing through eastern Oregon, giving speeches, missing meals now and then, and how he and Gerry appreciated the wonderful food, laying lavish compliments on our hostess, Joan.

The inexpensive luncheon for the Senator proved to be a win-win occasion for the senator, the community leaders and Western Power.

We found our display booth at IEEE conventions was an excellent sales aid. It was certainly expensive, but in terms of exposure to all segments of our market, the benefits far outweighed the cost. Interestingly enough, nearly every day at our booth, someone would bring up the subject of the possibility of a stock sale or a merger.

Most of the time it was easy to recognize the wannabes from the real thing. One of the "real things" who never failed to come by for a visit was my friend Jim Zboyovsky, president of Kearney Division, Kearney National. Jim had inquired many times in the past regarding my plans for retirement.

"If and when we decide to sell, I will definitely promise you will be the first to know," I would tell him. I always invited Jim to stop by our Hood River Plant for a visit.

When Jim finally took me up on my invitation, he was with my friend Hank Schwager, president and founder of Powerdyne, a high voltage switch manufacturer in the Portland area. Hank had developed something new in high voltage switches—a vacuum switch, known in the trade as a VAC-PAC. Jim told me he was negotiating with Hank to merge Powerdyne with Kearney, and this soon came to pass. I escorted Jim and Hank on a tour through the plant and gave Jim product information for his file. As they left the plant, I was told a Dr. Paul Umeh from Nigeria was waiting to see me.

Paul, an officer of Imemba Brothers, a Nigerian international trading firm, was visiting the Northwest, and because of my activity in international trade, he was referred to me. His principal interest was in electrical distribution equipment, so we hit it off very well—meeting all afternoon at the plant, and in the evening over cocktails in our home overlooking the Columbia River.

"If there is an interest in your product developments in my country, would you consider a visit to Nigeria for engineering discussions?" he asked.

"If there is a possibility of business in Nigeria, I would be happy to discuss plans for a visit," I replied.

We had no word from Nigeria for two years, because of their unsettled political situation. Finally we received a letter containing an invitation to address engineering groups at their National Electrical Authority.

The letter was from Gabriel Ndubuka, supervisor of electrical distribution in Lagos. At the time the letter arrived, I was well along in preparation for a visit to Daharan, Saudi Arabia, to give some help to a new agent there. After checking my business schedule, I decided to combine the two visits into one long trip.

Leaving Daharan, Saudi Arabia, after a week-long visit, I flew to Amsterdam for an overnight stay, then a nonstop flight leaving the next afternoon for Lagos. Mr. Ndubuka indicated in his letter there would be a representative at the Lagos airport to meet me and drive me to a hotel provided by the Nigerian government. We took off in late afternoon and flew south over France and the Sahara desert. About halfway across the desert, the plane had to return to Amsterdam because of instrument trouble.

We landed at Schipol airport and were told to relax in their lounge until a replacement flight could be arranged. It was quite late, about 10:00 P.M., when we boarded the replacement flight and again headed to Lagos. This time the scenery over the Sahara had changed from sunshine to one gigantic thunderstorm. Lightning flashed from horizon to horizon, east to west. Finally, about 1:30 A.M., we landed in the rain and taxied to the small Lagos terminal.

A man was asleep on one of the benches in the terminal. He jumped up when the passengers trooped in and ran up to me like he knew me.

"Are you Mr. Bright? Mr. Ndubuka sent me to take you to the hotel," he said, and told me he would pick up my luggage—the hotel was ten miles away.

By the time we left, the terminal was deserted, and the rain continued coming straight down. There was no wind, just heavy rain with small lightning now and then. The highway to Lagos was two lanes and flat, through dreary, desolate countryside. A few miles down the highway, we encountered flashlights waving ahead of us in the roadway to stop us. Six men, who looked like thugs, armed with Uzi machineguns, surrounded the car, ordered us out for a search, opened the trunk, and started prying open my suitcase and the box of samples. My driver gave them a big argument in their native language, saying I was there by order of the government.

After more heated discussions, they let us go on our way. The last flashlight stop by armed guards was at the base of a long ramp leading up to the lighted city on the outskirts of Lagos. This time they demanded we open the suitcase and the box, while one man held his Uzi against the driver's heart. Once they had poked around inside the suitcase and box, we were told to leave—and went, soaked but unhindered, to the government-arranged hotel.

The driver told me the guards were looking for smuggled guns. Guns that would sell for $200 in the United States would bring $2,000 in Nigeria. The driver was not sure whether the men who stopped us were crooks or government employees.

The hotel lobby was very plain and empty. There was no one at the reception desk. Looking over the desk, we could see bare feet and someone asleep on the floor. We woke him up and registered, and the driver escorted me to my room on the second floor, along with my luggage. There was a fifty-five gallon drum of water on the walkway by the room door. In looking around the room, I questioned the need for the bucket in the bathroom.

The driver explained that water was quite scarce, and if I were to use the toilet facilities, I should get a bucket full of water from the barrel outside the room to flush the toilet. This was the hotel for official guests of the Nigerian government.

The driver was there at 8:00 A.M. next morning and took me to their headquarters, where we had rolls and coffee.

Next, we headed for Gabriel Ndubuka's office. An alert, sharp-looking Nigerian, Gabriel was a twenty-five year veteran in the utility and had served in electric power generation, distribution, and construction departments. He was at that time concerned with the Lagos electrical distribution department which, he said, was in terrible shape. He suggested a quick tour of the city, so that I could get a feel for their problems, then speak to engineer group meetings.

Our tour covered perhaps a square mile of the city, but it was enough to convince me that they did indeed have a huge power distribution problem. The one encouraging sign was their 30,000-volt primary power system, solidly built using modern methods and completely circling the city.

Their secondary electrical system, serving homes and businesses, was a British standard ring-bus, fifty-cycle system. Some of their switchgear enclosures were tipped over, others battered in. The area was in extreme poverty, and apparently vandalism and robbery were rampant. We passed through areas in the city where mothers were cooking food for their children over charcoal fires on the sidewalks.

The engineer meetings progressed, one before and two after a lunch break. The engineers were sharp, asking intelligent questions, asking that certain slides be reviewed, asking why our U.S. standards called for thus and so. It was my opinion, expressed to the groups, that the British equipment in use in their power system was designed for conditions in Great Britain and worked quite well there. However, I felt their local conditions called for vacuum switches and elbow-disconnect switches in fiberglass enclosures. Lots of nodding heads led me to believe that many of the engineers agreed with me.

Some of the discussion was about the fact that Lagos was in such a mess—requiring rebuilding of the water, power, and telephone systems,—hat the government had decided to develop a new capital city at Abuja, more inland and central for Nigeria's 100 million population. Engineering and construction were already under way. The engineering groups agreed that a Western Suburban substation would be sited near the entrance to the new city.

That evening Gabriel invited me to his home in Lagos, where his wife, Comfort, joined us in cocktails and pleasant conversation, comparing life in the United States to life in Nigeria. Their hometown was Umuahia, in the state of Imo. They talked about how strict tribal laws in the villages discourage theft, violence, and other illegal activity. We continued the evening with a lovely British dinner of roast beef with all the trimmings, served formally at their private club.

I have often reflected on the strange circumstance that people who are involved in operating electric utilities, from one end of the world to the other, seem to be all produced out of the same mold. They are usually pleasant, intelligent, respectable people.

The two-week Saudi Arabia/Nigeria trip was completed without a single travel hitch. It was very important to me to be able to keep business appointments over thousands of miles without the worry and hassle on how to get there, where to stay and so forth. How did we do it? No problem!

Our outstanding travel agent, Dolores Habberstad, owner of Hazel Phillips Travel Service, had for over two decades arranged frequent trips for us around the United States and foreign countries. Her modern computerized operation, programmed with our travel preferences, had allowed her and her staff always to get us there and back at the lowest cost and without problems.

21

The Business of Selling a Business

Time went by very fast, probably because I enjoyed my family life and my work. The passing of time became evident to me when I was working on our corporate agenda for the year 1983. It was twenty-five years earlier that we had incorporated Western Power Products, when I was forty years old. My career goals included the objectives of starting my own business by age forty, and retiring after building a successful business, around the age of sixty-five. To voluntarily step out of a business you have built and enjoyed is a bit like losing an old friend. During 1983 I would begin making plans to step out of the business; and during 1983 I lost my oldest, best friend, Bill Wild.

The ship repair facility in Portland where Bill had worked since our arrival more than forty years before had closed their Portland yard and moved to a new ship repair facility in San Diego, where Bill continued doing what he liked best as the general manager.

His wife, Alice, told me later that one day in March 1983 he came home to their apartment for lunch, and while driving back to his office, he suffered a fatal heart attack.

Bill and I never talked much about death, but once he remarked that when his time came to go, he hoped he would "die with his boots on." At least he avoided a long terminal illness. His passing canceled the retirement plans we had discussed years earlier.

As teenagers, we made a pact to help each other achieve our career goals. I am sure our constant support, encouragement, and concern for each other's success, particularly during our early years, made it possible for both of us to achieve our separate lifetime goals. Even though our final careers were different, our work style and management awareness, working together in the same companies for eleven years, created momentum that supported each of us to our career goals.

The realization in 1982 that my sixty-fifth birthday had arrived was not a personal shock, but the realization that the time had come when plans must be made for my departure from the company was a big jolt. This should be no big deal, I reminded myself. My career objectives have been realized, so now it's time to get on with my life after business.

As much as one part of my conscience accepted the logic of my approaching retirement, another part resisted the thought of stepping out of an activity I really enjoyed. My position in the company was not really work to me.

We had subscribed to an industry publication, *The Business Owner*, for some years. Their columns, often written by recognized authorities in their field, had been helpful to me in forming some of my past decisions, so the copies were always filed after I read them. Certain copies of *Inc.* magazine were also helpful and were filed. The question then in my mind was just what the fair market value of our company would be if we should decide to sell.

There are lots of books written on the subject, and I read a few, but most helpful to me was a review of the many articles relating to the process of establishing the market value of a company in *The Business Owner* from 1980 to 1984. My objective was to establish a fair market value for the sale of all corporate assets, using generally accepted methods of arriving at market value.

Preliminary estimates of fair market value of the company, surprisingly, were well up in the seven figures. The value came as a surprise because we never had any reason to think of selling the company in the previous twenty-odd years. Our efforts always had been directed toward building a successful company, not putting something together to make a million dollars. The preliminary figures showed over a million dollars in surplus cash—thanks partly to the steady stewardship of our cash flow by our comptroller, Lynn Beier.

Any consideration of changes in corporate policy or control had to take the shareholders into consideration. After all, shareholders were owners of part of the corporation and had certain legal rights. It was to my great advantage, however, to own over 50 percent of all issued stock through the years, so that I could control the destiny of the company. Approaching retirement, now the scenario for me would not be a speech of congratulations, a round of applause, and perhaps a gold watch, as it would be for an employee of a large corporation. It would be up to me to decide my future and the future of the company.

After a meeting of the minds with family members, we established a policy that would ultimately result in my complete retirement from the company, and would protect the rights of shareholders. I preferred to seek a negotiated sale, merger or other arrangement, rather than listing the company for sale with a brokerage. The best way to resolve the problem was to have a series of meetings with our management team, discuss the alternatives, and arrive at a viable solution.

After giving considerable thought to how a company sale should be structured, I considered a public stock offering, a sale to employees by leveraged buy-out, or a sale to employees by an employee stock ownership plan (ESOP). Also considered was the sale of company assets only versus a sale of all corporate stock. I considered merger with a switchgear manufacturer, the sale of my personal stock to an investor, or hiring a company manager while I retained my stock—or to defer all sale activity for five years.

The first option, consideration of a public stock offering, seemed to be a good first step to determine whether a market existed for a public offering. I was acquainted with Larry Black of Black & Company, Investment Bankers. After assembling several year-end reports, federal and state tax reports, catalogs, sales projections, and so forth, we arranged a meeting. We discussed the company, our market, growth projections, and so on. Larry asked to keep the data for his review.

A few weeks later Larry reported that, in his opinion, it was not a good time to make an initial public offering of our stock. He had consulted with other investment bankers, and all agreed the timing was bad, and it would be best if we waited a year or two. The market considered electric utilities to be a "mature" industry—not much prospect for growth in earnings for electric utility suppliers.

A sale to employees by leveraged buy-out was an option we looked into very carefully. Our local bank had handled our account for some years and reviewed our operating statements and earning projections. The bank offered to loan the proposed management group a seven-figure amount to buy out my stock, subject to the management group pledging their personal assets to repay the loan. There was reluctance by some in the group to assume the financial liability, to be backed with corporate assets and their personal assets.

It was true that all during the preceding twenty-five years, I had backed our bank credit line with all my personal assets, but this was quite a different scenario. A future inverse business cycle lasting for a period of time could raise havoc with earning projections, resulting in possible default and loss of personal and corporate assets. And to further complicate the leveraged buy-out idea, Jim Coon had plans to retire early. A key man in operations, Jim would not be easy to replace.

After reviewing all options, our management group settled on the sale of all corporate stock as the solution that best fit our organization. The other options were solutions for some people facing retirement. The option of a sale after waiting for another five years had been selected by some we read about, resulting in their heirs trying to muddle through a sale after the original owners died.

In April 1984 we discussed my retirement decision with our board of directors; the options had been reviewed by management in some detail, and we made our conclusions. We would prepare to look for a company to purchase our corporate stock. After a discussion, we voted to approve the stock sale option, and to provide the management team a better chance of continuing to manage the new company. We voted to name Jim Coon executive vice president, Lynn Beier treasurer, vice president, and assistant to the president, and Larry Sanguras vice president of operations.

By mid-1984 we had established our idea of a fair market value for the company. We had substantial factual data to back up our numbers, which included a five-year record of sales and profit margins of all our products, plus projections of sales for the future five years. Lynn had prepared a very complete file detailing all of the corporate assets and liabilities, and all of the basic information about the company that a serious prospective buyer might want to know.

In arriving at our seven-figure market value for the company, we used several valuation methods, including the widely used multiple of five times annual pre-tax profits. We included equity in our real estate, property, equipment and molds. Patents had no asset value as patents. The patent certificate was considered as an asset only as a "good will" item, so any money a purchaser would pay for patents would have to be written off as expense.

However, our favorable profit margins on several product lines were possible only because of our patents, so we assigned an annual dollar amount as the value we felt should be credited to patent protection, and applied a multiple of five to arrive at a six-figure patent valuation.

In June 1984 we were in Washington, D.C., for an industry meeting and decided to drop into Atlanta to visit Kearney headquarters. Jim Zboyovsky, president of Kearney Division, was in his office to greet me, along with our friend Jack Williamson, the marketing manager. We had a long discussion about the decision to sell the company, and as promised some years earlier, we were giving Kearney notice of our asking price, terms, and conditions. Jim said he would report to their headquarters and get back to us within the next few months.

Jim had a tight schedule for the next few months, and it was January 1985 before we could arrange a lunch in Portland for more discussions, and later a short meeting at the airport. However, in

March Jim spent a day with us at our plant, followed by a visit from Jack Williamson and Mr. Milas in April. In June we met with Jim's boss, Mr. Aricio, and two of his staff in our conference room, followed by a dinner meeting. Their visit clearly was an attempt by the Kearney executives to do some bargain-hunting, to be expected in a sales preliminary. The talk was about a sale using "earn-out" formulas, installment payments based on future earnings, and so forth. It was a very exasperating day, but we all kept our cool and were polite but firm in rejecting their proposals.

In July, Jim spent another full day at our plant, reviewing some details and asking questions resulting from previous discussions. Jim promised Kearney would make a firm offer by August 15, 1985. The Kearney people, it seemed to me, were having trouble understanding our products and the scope of our business. Although they would not admit it, some of their questions spoke volumes about their lack of knowledge of the electric utility market, particularly details of underground power distribution, packaged substations, and so forth.

On August 15, we received a phone call from Mr. Jaffe at Kearney regarding their price offer. His message was that it would be necessary for their company to postpone their discussions with us due to conflicts that had come up in other parts of their business, which would take all of their time and attention.

We received a phone call in January 1986 from my friend Don at Westinghouse, advising that Westinghouse was doing some restructuring and could not become involved in a purchase for some time. After hearing our asking price, he asked how many shares of stock we had outstanding, and the next question was how many shares I owned.

"My God, Bill, if you get your asking price you'll be a multi-millionaire," he said after I answered. I told Don that we probably would get our asking price, because the business was fairly priced. We had no further contact with Westinghouse. The word on the street was that Don had later joined another firm.

Our long-time friend, Bob McFarlane, our CPA and board member for many years, called me to discuss the Kearney purchase offer. Bob asked if I would have any objection to him calling Jim

Zboyovsky at Kearney to see if they intended to make another offer. I assured Bob we would have no objection. His call to Jim must have had some "moxie," because a few days later Jim called to say Kearney in fact did have another offer, which was on the agenda for their next board meeting, and he would get back to me as soon as the board acted.

It was early June when we next heard from Jim with a new offer to purchase our company. Their board had approved a package of price, terms and conditions, which was very close to our requirements.

"We're happy to receive your offer Jim, but we've been in serious discussion with Kearney since June 1985. If Kearney can proceed with the final details, so that we can plan a closing by the end of July, we're ready to proceed with Kearney," I said. "However, if you are not prepared to proceed on this time basis, we feel obligated to continue with other companies who've indicated an interest in purchasing the company."

Jim assured me they would move promptly, and scheduled a meeting within days between their attorneys and our attorney Don McEwen, and Allen Bush, a tax attorney in the law firm.

The meeting of attorneys took place in McEwen's offices on July 1. The final demands were argued and argued, finally arriving at a point where I announced it seemed pointless to continue the meeting. At this, Jim Zboyovsky asked if he and I could caucus privately. We left the room and in no time settled our problems. Jim assured me the final papers would be drawn up to suit our requirements, and we agreed to a final closing to be held in Don McEwen's office on August 1, 1986.

Jim arrived at our plant later in July for an inspection and review, called "due diligence"—a means of assuring stockholders of the purchasing company that their funds were being invested prudently.

The big day of final closing came as scheduled. Reams of papers provided by the attorneys were in stacks on McEwen's conference table for the principals to sign. When the last signatures were in place, it was time for Kearney to deliver the check, time for shaking hands, warm compliments exchanged, and photos taken of the principals (Plate 17). Don and Allen broke out a giant bottle of champagne.

It was very fitting for the final closing to take place in Don's office. Over two decades as corporate secretary and board member, Don was involved in all of our corporate board decisions through the years, much to our benefit. And it was Allen Bush, a tax attorney and member of Don's firm, who handled all of our personal legal matters for years.

The signing ceremony was completed and the check deposited in the bank. Now it was time for Jim and his wife Lil, and Joan and I, to relax on the deck of our home in Hood River overlooking the peaceful scene of the Columbia River and Mount Adams—a great spot for the four of us to unwind over cocktails. Following a leisurely dinner at the beautiful Columbia Gorge Hotel, Jim and Lil left for their hotel in Portland and then back to Atlanta.

Some have asked why we chose to handle the sale of our company in-house, rather than listing the company with a brokerage, the usual procedure. Once we decided we would sell the company in the near future, we immediately started learning ways to establish fair market value of a closely held company as outlined earlier. Since we were strong in a niche of the electric utility industry, we knew personally many of the manufacturers in the industry. We knew where our product line could enhance another manufacturer's product line for greater coverage. Therefore there was little a brokerage firm could do for us as far as contacts in the U.S. market were concerned.

The contract of sale to Kearney included employment contracts with Jim Coon as plant manager, and Lynn Beier as accountant/office manager for five years. Also, I would be a consultant to Kearney for five years. All three contracts included a "non-compete" clause to prevent us, if we had the urge, from setting up a competing company.

The reasons I have written this true life career story are two.

The first reason is to show that it is indeed possible for individuals from low-income families to find a job after high school, to attend night classes, and to advance rapidly to better jobs and higher responsibilities.

The second concerns a career as an entrepreneur. A recent survey showed that 70 percent of individuals contacted—ages twenty-two to thirty-two—would prefer having their own business. However, surveys a few years ago claimed 85 percent of entrepreneurs fail within the first five years as a result of lack of real business world preparation.

Working in a job in the industry of choice for five to ten years to gather first-hand knowledge, in addition to following proven standards of personal savings, establishing bank credit, and selecting professional advisors, will greatly improve the entrepreneur's chances of success.

The life of an entrepreneur is not for everyone, but it surely was the life for me. From that first day when we incorporated Western Power Products on January 9, 1958, until final closing of the sale to Kearney National on August 1, 1986, operation of the company was a continuing challenge. Almost every day was a different scenario, and I met an ever-widening circle of business acquaintances and friends, ultimately extending around the world. And above all, I felt a tremendous sense of accomplishment, demonstrating once again that the American dream is here for all of us, if we play by the rules of the game. We all have the opportunity, regardless of wealth or social status.

To order additional copies of

Two Bills from Boston

Book: $15.95   Shipping/Handling: $3.50

Contact

Bill Bright
~~P.O. Box 1507~~
Portland OR   97207

Phone   503-242-0733
Fax   503-242-0248
E-mail   billbright@aol.com

SAUGUS PUBLIC LIBRARY
295 CENTRAL ST.
SAUGUS, MA 01906